Top Secrets for Doing Your Own Pr

A TOP SECRETS BOOK

TOP SECRETS FOR DOING YOUR OWN PR

BY GINI GRAHAM SCOTT, PH.D.

AUTHOR OF A DOZEN BOOKS
ON WORK AND PROFESSIONAL
DEVELOPMENT, INCLUDING *WANT IT,
SEE IT, GET IT!* AND *ENJOY! 101 LITTLE
WAYS TO ADD FUN TO YOUR WORK
EVERYDAY*

WWW.GINIGRAHAMSCOTT.COM
WWW.PRANDNETWORKINGCONNECTION.COM

ASJA PRESS
NEW YORK   BLOOMINGTON

TOP SECRETS FOR DOING YOUR OWN PR

ASJA Press
an imprint of iUniverse, Inc.

iUniverse books may be ordered through booksellers or by contacting:

iUniverse
1663 Liberty Drive
Bloomington, IN 47403
www.iuniverse.com
1-800-Authors (1-800-288-4677)

Because of the dynamic nature of the Internet, any Web addresses or links contained in this book may have changed since publication and may no longer be valid.

ISBN: 978-1-4502-0460-6 (sc)

Printed in the United States of America

iUniverse rev. date: 02/18/2010

CONTENTS

INTRODUCTION..**xi**

HOW YOU CAN DO YOUR OWN PR.....................................xi

MY OWN BACKGROUND AND HOW
I HAVE GOTTEN PUBLICITY xii

CHAPTER 1: LAUNCHING YOUR PR CAMPAIGN............. 1

CREATING YOUR CAMPAIGN THEME 1

DETERMINING YOUR TARGET MARKET......................... 2

LINKING YOUR PRODUCT OR SERVICE
TO THE DAILY NEWS.. 2

PROMOTING A NICHE PRODUCT OR SERVICE............. 3

USING PROMOTIONAL EVENTS 3

    Using Celebrities... 3

    Finding Low Cost Venues for Your Events............................... 4

USING THE SOCIAL MEDIA 4

CHAPTER 2: WAYS TO APPROACH THE PRESS 7

USING A PERSONAL AND LOCAL APPROACH 7

    Deciding on Who Will Contact the Media............................ 7

    Building from Local to National PR.................................... 8

    Contacting the Local Media 9

TIPS FOR GETTING THROUGH TO THE MEDIA............. 9

Using Your Initial Call as a Door Opener 9

Getting Past the Receptionist 10

Sending an Initial Query by E-Mail 10

Using Your Media Contact's Preferences 11

Tying Your Story to the Latest News 11

The Power of Buzz and Referrals 12

Gaining Interest from Radio and TV Stations. 12

CHAPTER 3: CREATING YOUR PRESS MATERIALS 15

CREATING A PRESS KIT AND PRESS RELEASE 15

Sending Out a Press Release or Query Letter 15

WHAT TO INCLUDE IN A PRESS RELEASE 16

Headline or Subject Line 16

Using a Subhead 17

"For Immediate Release" Introduction 17

Writing Your Release Like a News Story 17

Contact Information 18

The Difference Between a Press Release, Query Letter, and
Social Media Posting 18

Finding Contacts to Send Your Release or Query Letter 19

CREATING A PRESS KIT 20

Selecting Items to Use in Your Press Kit 21

Types of Presentation Folders to Use 22

Sending Your Press Kit by E-Mail 22

When to Send Out Your Material 23

CHAPTER 4: USING A WEBSITE OR BLOG IN YOUR PR
CAMPAIGN 25

USING A WEBSITE FOR PROMOTION 25

Using Search Engine Optimization and Keywords to Increase
Website Traffic 26

Using Your City to Target Your Market 27

Using Flash on Your Website 27

WRITING A BLOG 27

Turning Your Blog Into an Article 28

Pitching Your Article to the Print Media 28

Turning Blogs from Articles to E-Books and POD Books 29

Frequency, Length, and Format for a Blog 29

CHAPTER 5: SENDING YOUR PRESS MATERIALS TO THE MEDIA.. 31

PR RELEASE AND POSTING SERVICES............................ 31
PR DATABASE SERVICES.. 32
DOING YOUR OWN E-MAIL BLAST 33

CHAPTER 6: THE IMPORTANCE OF FOLLOW-UP 35

MAKING FAVORABLE CONTACTS.................................. 35
PR RELEASE FOLLOW UPS... 36

CHAPTER 7: TIMING YOUR PRESS CAMPAIGN 39

CHAPTER 8: KEEPING TRACK OF YOUR PR 41

WHEN TO EXPECT YOUR STORY TO APPEAR................ 41
TRACKING THE PR YOU SEND AND
THE PUBLICITY YOU GET.. 42

CHAPTER 9: GETTING YOUR WORK PUBLISHED 43

WRITING ARTICLES FOR PUBLICATION 43
  Deciding Whether to Offer Articles for Free or Pay 43
  Using an Article for Promotional Purposes 44
  Typical Payment for Articles 44
  Using a PR Release to Offer Your Articles for Publication........ 46
PUBLISHING YOUR ARTICLES ON EZINES..................... 46

CHAPTER 10: USING E-BOOKS TO PROMOTE YOUR PRODUCT OR SERVICE.............................. 49

THE IMPORTANCE OF E-BOOKS..................................... 49
COPYRIGHT PROTECTION 50
MARKETING AND DISTRIBUTING YOUR E-BOOK 51
  Selling an E-Book in a PDF Format 51
  Selling Your E-Book through an Online Reader 52
PUBLISHING YOUR E-BOOK AS A
PRINT-ON DEMAND BOOK 52
THE FORMAT FOR AN E-BOOK....................................... 53

CHARGING FOR E-BOOKS 53
WAYS TO PUT YOUR E-BOOK TOGETHER 55
PUBLISHING AND DISTRIBUTING YOUR E-BOOK 57
FINDING A MAINSTREAM PUBLISHER 57

CHAPTER 11: CREATING A PACKAGE OF MATERIALS . 59
USING AUDIOBOOKS AND VIDEOS 59
CREATING A COMBINATION PACKAGE 60

CHAPTER 12: NETWORKING EVENTS 61
CREATING YOUR OWN NETWORKING EVENTS 61
Some Examples of Successful Events 61
Organizing Your Own Social Event 62
Setting Up a Promotional Workshop or Seminar 62
Attending Networking Events 63
Being Prepared Anytime 63
A Caution on Promoting MLM Products and Services 64
Participating in Referral Clubs 65
Participating in Entrepreneurial Organizations, Conferences, and Meetings 66
Getting Tables at Networking Events and Conferences 67

CHAPTER 13: USING THE SOCIAL MEDIA 69
The Major Social Media Sites 69
The Importance of Building a Relationship 69
Posting Your Information on Multiple Sites 70
Joining Groups in Your Field 70
Combining the Social Media with Other Networking 71

CHAPTER 14: WORKING WITH OTHERS IN YOUR PR CAMPAIGN 73
DOING JOINT PR WITH OTHERS 73
USING AND CHOOSING A PR PROFESSIONAL 74
Making Your Decision 74
Cutting Down Your PR Costs in Working with a Pro 75
Getting Quotes and Weighing Alternatives 75

Working with PR People Locally or at a Distance...................76

CHAPTER 15: ASSESSING YOUR PR CAMPAIGN 79

THE IMPORTANCE OF TIMING.. 79
BEING READY TO RESPOND AND
MAKE NEEDED CHANGES 80
KEEPING TRACK OF YOUR PR RESULTS......................... 80
Deciding If Your Campaign Is Working or Not..................... 80
Ways to Track Your Results.. 81
CHECKING THE TRAFFIC TO YOUR WEBSITE 82
THE COSTS OF A PR CAMPAIGN 83
Different Types of Arrangements 83
The Duration and Costs of a PR Campaign 84
DOING A COST BENEFIT ANALYIS 84
Factors to Consider 84
The Length of Time for the Assessment................................. 85
Making Your Decision... 86

CHAPTER 16: EXPANDING YOUR PR CAMPAIGN 87

USING THE PR YOU GET TO GAIN
ADDITIONAL MEDIA EXPOSURE...................................... 87
CREATING A UNIQUE IDENTITY F
OR YOUR COMPANY 88

CHAPTER 17: WHEN TO CUT BACK YOUR PR............... 89

PROMOTING THE UNDIFFERENTIATED
PRODUCT OR SERVICE 89
PROMOTING THE SPECIALIZED PRODUCT
OR SERVICE 90

OTHER BOOKS BY THE AUTHOR....................................... 91

AUTHOR CONTACT INFORMATION............................. 93

INTRODUCTION

How You Can Do Your Own Pr

TOP SECRETS FOR DOING YOUR OWN PR is based on a series of workshops I have given on how to promote any kind of product or service yourself. This is a way to keep your costs down, rather than hiring a PR firm, which typically charges a $2000-5000 monthly retainer for a campaign which commonly lasts about 3-4 months. If you can afford it, an established PR firm can draw on its connections to get you publicity. But if you don't have such funds, you can use these techniques to do your own publicity.

Today you can do your own PR more easily and inexpensively than ever. You can do everything from sending out press releases and query letters to the traditional media to creating a social media campaign to using online organizations like Meetup to build a quick following.

Publicity is less expensive and more powerful than just placing an ad, because people know you have paid for an ad. So you have more credibility when your publicity campaign generates a news story. Thus, the more you can spread the word through publicity rather than advertising, the more that will help you promote your product or service, though sometimes advertising can open the door to your getting publicity, such as when somebody buys a big ad and that becomes a compelling story, because people respond to that ad in a powerful way. The Apple "1984" ad is a powerful example of this phenomena. The commercial only aired once, but it was picked up by the media and created so much buzz for Apple that there was no need to pay to run it again.

DO YOUR OWN PR covers the major types of PR you can do on your own. It draws on my experience in doing promotional campaigns for several dozen books, as well as dozens of workshops, seminars, and classes I have attended on public relations and publicity. I also gathered material for this program through teaching a grad school class on PR and marketing at the University of Notre Dame de Namur. And I have had numerous discussions with writers and company owners about what they did that was successful in their own PR campaigns.

My Own Background And How I Have Gotten Publicity

First, let me introduce myself to show what I have done that qualifies me to write this book about doing your own PR. I've been a writer, consultant, speaker, and seminar/workshop leader, mainly doing programs based on my books for the last 30 years. I've published over 50 books, and have worked with publishers or on my own in promoting them. In addition, I have published about two dozen games and assisted some game manufacturers in promoting these games. My latest books include: WANT IT, SEE IT, GET IT! and ENJOY! 101 LITTLE WAYS TO ADD FUN TO YOUR WORK EVERYDAY.

Promoting my own books has been an especially powerful learning experience, because now you not only use the mainstream media, but you have to develop social media campaigns, too, to create a presence on the major sites, which include LinkedIn, Facebook, and Twitter.

At one time publishers used to invest in major PR campaigns for their authors. But now, unless you're famous already as a celebrity, are in a big news story, or are involved in the latest scandal of the day, you generally have to do your own PR. So that's how I learned a lot about PR, and for my last book, the publisher's publicist and my editor sent me all of this information about getting on LinkedIn, Facebook, and Twitter. Besides that, I've written and sent press releases to the major media, and I've been on hundreds of radio and TV shows, including Oprah and Montel Williams.

In writing books, my specialty is business and work relationships, and professional and personal development. I've chosen to highlight a few specialties, because the media wants people who are experts in something. They don't like it when you do a lot of different things, because you may seem scattered. So it's important to pick your strongest topic and emphasize that. In turn, having this expertise helps you develop a high profile, called a "platform", which is what publishers, agents, and managers are looking for.

Building that platform is like a circle, in which the more publicity you get, the more you build that platform; and the more powerful your platform, the easiest it is to get PR. So the more PR you get for whatever you do, the more that will help you sell your projects or services, as well as get an even bigger platform. The key is to get the ball rolling and build on that, which is what I've been doing in promoting my books, games, and other projects.

Recently, I've gotten into e-book publishing, too – not only writing my own books but helping clients write theirs, because E-Books are a powerful way to gain credibility, whatever your field. Traditional publishers are now more and more hesitant to offer a deal unless you're already famous or have a platform.

So it may make sense to initially write and publish your own E-Book, rather than wait for a deal with a traditional publisher. That way you can publish your own e-book much more quickly and do the kind of promotion you would do for mainstream publishers. But when you do it yourself, you will gain a much higher return from sales. With a mainstream book, you only get a 10-15 % royalty based on the net or a hard cover price, whereas if you publish an e-book and do the same amount of publicity, you make much more money per sale yourself – generally about 30-60%, depending on your mark-up on the book and whether you sell through a wholesaler, retailer, or direct to the customer.

Another way I've gotten publicity is through a 6-year old company I sold in October 2008 that connects writers and others to publishers, agents, the film industry, and the media by sending a mass e-mail release or query letter. This mass approach is different from what PR agents do, since they commonly have a selected list of contacts that they contact or they locate people they want to contact and do so through personal contacts, phone calls, and personal e-mails.

However, the mass approach can also do personalized mailings using a special software that personalizes each e-mail and a dedicated mailer server to send e-mails to about 5,000 people in an hour. You select the media (such as radio, newspapers, TV, magazines, and the Internet media) and the type of interests (such as health, business or science). Then, the software sends it to the contacts in that type of media with that interest. Though I sold the business, I'm still helping the company by making these contacts with the media for clients.

CHAPTER 1: LAUNCHING YOUR PR CAMPAIGN

CREATING YOUR CAMPAIGN THEME

Start your campaign by developing your campaign theme. This theme is something you can sum up in a phrase or sentence, much like the title of a book. Think of your theme like a news story headline – it's a statement to quickly attract consumer interest.

For example, when Apple first brought out the Apple computer, their campaign focused around the notion of being different from the PC – it was the computer for "the rest of us." Other examples of a theme are Verizon's campaign of "having more phones in the network than any other service" or "having a more reliable network with fewer dropped calls than any other network."

You can have multiple campaigns, but for each one, center your message around that theme. It's like having a headline and subheads. Then you tell the story in the rest of your message.

The particular theme you choose should also be one that resonates with your selected target market.

DETERMINING YOUR TARGET MARKET

Your target market is the group of consumers who will be most receptive to your product or service. Your campaign theme should appeal to them. You thus need a match between your message and the group it is aimed at.

Don't think your product or service will appeal to everyone. That's too broad. Focus on the segments of the market which will be most receptive. Then, that focus will help you determine the best media and approach to use to reach that market.

This analysis of your market may mean you should review the name you have picked for your product, service, or PR campaign. Maybe you might want to choose a better or more compelling name or even use different names to appeal to different markets. So be ready to go back and reconsider your initial choices if necessary.

This willingness to review and revise is crucial, because sometimes you may think you have chosen a great name. But if you do some market research and get feedback, you may discover that others don't relate to or like the name. So it may be better to change it early on than to hope you can change people's attitudes and opinions, which are often difficult to change.

LINKING YOUR PRODUCT OR SERVICE TO THE DAILY NEWS

If you can tie your product or service to what's going on in the news, that can help you get publicity, because your product or service seems more timely and relevant, rather than just another new product, service, book, or whatever. So look at what's happening in the news and how can you be an expert to comment on what's happening or how your product or service might provide an important and unique benefit.

For instance, if you want to promote a humanitarian song, rather than directly promoting the song, promote some of the ways the song been used in different groups or how the song's message ties into something in the news, such as promoting awareness of the immigration crisis which is very much in the news.

PROMOTING A NICHE PRODUCT OR SERVICE

If you have a niche product or service, figure out what is your niche market, so you can direct your PR towards that market. By the same token, pick out key words to appeal to that market, and any time you do a mass mailing, feature those words in the mailing. Likewise, pick the particular media that serve that market.

For instance, if you have a product or book that appeals to managers, direct your PR to the business media. If it is a product or book that appeals to women consumers, direct your PR towards consumer publications or feature editors who cover topics that appeal to women. The more you can target the media, the better it is for your product or service.

USING PROMOTIONAL EVENTS

One way to promote your product and services is to create a special promotional event around it. Some ways to do this are:

- Create tie-ins with other groups, so you might do something on a larger scale.

- Contribute part of your earnings for the event or product sales to a charity, whereby a certain percentage goes to that charity.

- Put on a free event so that people in the media would feel more comfortable promoting it because it's free. If you are charging, say $10 at the door, even if that's to cover your costs for food and supplies, the media will think it's a commercial event which you should advertise. So to maximize your publicity appeal, make your event free.

- Find a way to make your event stand out and be unique.

Using Celebrities

Because we're in a very celebrity-driven culture, if you can get a celebrity or a high-profile spokesperson to appear at your event or endorse your products or service, you'll increase your credibility and appeal. Sometimes celebrities will appear at an event or provide an endorsement for free, if they really like what you're doing. Other times they may want a certain fee or percentage of the door charge or of sales.

If your event or the sales potential is a large enough, a percentage of the door or sales may be all you need and you may not have to offer a guarantee or pay out anything upfront. Or connecting your event or sales to a charity may help you build sales as well as get celebrity endorsements, since some celebrities pick out charities they are particularly interested in. So if you can connect your event or activity to a charity that may be a way to gain the participation of a celebrity who is committed to that cause.

Finding Low Cost Venues for Your Events

Often you can find restaurants and hotels for your event for a low price or free, because the restaurant or hotel expects increased business from the people you bring.

For example, I did some events at the Monsoon Café on the Promenade in Santa Monica with about 100 people at each event, and they only required a $100 payment for the use of a large banquet hall and a $100 guarantee for the bartender's tips. Most of what we collected at the door -- $10 each – went to buy hors d'oeuvres for the group. So the payments from the attendees easily covered the $100 fee, plus most people bought drinks, which reimbursed the bartender. So it was a win-win for all.

Now, due to the recession, many restaurants and bars are hurting, so they are more likely to give you the space for nothing, if it looks like you will bring them a large number of customers.

USING THE SOCIAL MEDIA

Using the social media like LinkedIn, Facebook, and Twitter, has become an important part of any PR campaign. A first step is putting up a compelling profile. Then, proactively build connections to let people know what you are doing, get them to come to your page, and promote special events.

Your first level connections are your direct connections and your second level are the people they are connected to, so your network can grow exponentially. For example, on LinkedIn I have about 250 first level connections now and nearly 4 million second level connections. But it's most important to get the first level connections, because these are the people who will get your initial announcements or invitations to your events, and then they may pass on this information or not.

One way to build your connections, suggested by a social media consultant specializing in LinkedIn, is to get cards from the people you meet at business networking events and inite them to join you on LinkedIn. That's what he does after every business or networking event he attends. Then, he adds in the cards from people he has just met and e-mails them an invitation to join LinkedIn or asks if he can send them an invitation to join.

However, as he suggests, be cautious in how you send out these invitations. Don't immediately invite people if you just picked up their card and weren't able to develop a personal connection. Rather, ask them if you can invite them or if they would like to invite you to connect. For example, write to people and say, "I'd like to invite you to become my linked-in partner, may I do so? Or you can send me an invitation to invite me." So you can connect either way. You can send them an invitation or they can send you an invitation.

This approach takes a little longer, since you send or receive the invite in two steps rather then inviting the person to connect to you right away. But it's better to use this two-step process with people you don't know well or at all, because if you invite too many people who say "I don't know you," you might get banned or suspended from the LinkedIn site. So you avoid the potential for being dropped from the social media site for spamming others.

If you have profiles on Facebook or Twitter, you can do much the same thing in inviting people to be your friend or follower.

But on these and other social media sites, too, as in building any relationship, it's a good idea to take it slow. So after you join, don't just immediately start promoting yourself or your company. Rather, start a conversation first, so you develop an ongoing relationship and trust, such as by sending useful tips or links to stories the other person may find of interest.

Often the first thing people do after joining one of these networks and creating a profile is to send out a promotional announcement about themselves. But such fast and aggressive promotional pitching can turn people off. So it's best to start developing a relationship before you launch a big promotional campaign. This way you build trust. Though using this approach can take longer to execute, it's worth doing, because when you start promoting your events and products and service, people will trust you and be more receptive.

CHAPTER 2:
WAYS TO APPROACH
THE PRESS

Depending on what you are promoting and your budget, you might use either a personal and local approach, a large scale media approach, or a combination of both. The local approach is especially appropriate if you are promoting a local business or service; the large scale approach makes more sense if you have a product or service that has national appeal.

USING A PERSONAL AND LOCAL APPROACH

How do you decide who will contact the media and how? Here are some suggestions.

Deciding on Who Will Contact the Media

There are several ways to use a personal and local approach and keep your costs down, including hiring a new publicist or a student intern, or acting as your own publicist. Here are the main considerations to think about.

Hiring a publicist who is just starting can be a good idea, since a new publicist may work for a fairly low hourly rate to build a track record. Such a person may be especially eager and do a good job, because they are looking for references.

Another good way to keep your costs down on a local campaign is to hire a student assistant from a local college or high school who is learning to do marketing and PR, and sometimes you can get them to work as unpaid interns on these projects. Sometimes you can find these students through a local jobs for students program in your city.

For instance, in Oakland, there is a Mayor's Summer Jobs program which helps high school seniors find work in local businesses, and I hired several interns through these programs, some of whom still work for me now that they are in college. Usually you can start with $7-8 an hour for students who are looking for their first job.

While students may not have the skills of a trained professional PR person, they can really do a good job if you have routine type of work, such as creating databases, finding information on the Internet, or making informational phone calls. If you have very detailed administrative type work, somebody who's quiet and shy might be a perfect person for that. If you have a lot of phoning and public contact work and the detail is less important, look for somebody who's outgoing. Though sometimes, one person can do both types of tasks.

Posing as your own publicist is another way to keep costs down, if you have an outgoing persuasive personality. In this case, instead of calling up and saying: "I've got this great product and service," you act as your publicist and say "I'm calling on behalf of this company or organization." Then, you can talk about how it's a really great company or organization or has this great new product or service. If you strike a chord, you might add: "So if you're interested, I can send you information."

The advantage of calling for yourself, rather than as you, is this puts a remove between you and the pitch for your company, product, or service, and it gives you more credibility. It sounds like you have somebody working for you or speaking for you, which makes whatever you are promoting sound more important and impressive, than if it's just you promoting you.

Building from Local to National PR

This local approach can help you build your campaign, so after you get a local story, it can help you get a larger story. The way this works is that sometimes this local story will get picked up by the other media, which has someone watching for local stories with broad national appeal.

So something can start out as a small story somewhere, and then it gets blown up into something big because of its broader appeal. Or sometimes you can leverage this story yourself by adding it to your press portfolio or sending a copy of the local article to other media.

Contacting the Local Media

Getting this local coverage can be an easy way to get started. Just contact an editor or reporter at your local daily or weekly paper by phone, fax, or e-mail or a combination of these approaches. Some editors and reporters will be receptive to a quick call where you give a one or two sentence pitch to get them intrigued. Then, you say more if they are interested or follow-up with an e-mail or fax with more information. Or you may find the e-mail of the editor or reporter you want to contact on the paper's masthead and send an e-mail. Then, if you get no response within a day or two, follow up with a phone call.

Typically, the editor assigns the piece, but if you get interest from a reporter, the reporter can suggest it to the editor and then get the assignment.

When you make the local call or send your initial e-mail, this is when you might have your assistant – or you posing as your assistant - make the initial call or sign the fax or e-mail to open the door to getting media interest. Then, if a reporter or editor wants to talk to you, go ahead and do so; just sound like you're somebody else if you previously posed as your assistant in making the initial contact.

TIPS FOR GETTING THROUGH TO THE MEDIA

Using Your Initial Call as a Door Opener

A good way to use your initial call is as a door opener, where you take about 30-45 seconds to quickly pitch your story. Later, as you have other stories to pitch (which might be a new approach to your product or service or tie-in with another news event), you can build a relationship based on mutual benefits.

If the media contact expresses interest after your initial phone call, follow up with a press release, query letter, press kits, or whatever they would like to see. You should have these press materials ready to send or be able to get these materials together within a day or two of your call.

Initially don't send out a full press kit to everyone in the media group you are contacting. It can be very expensive. Also, it's best to first see if the contact wants the press kit and what he or she wants to see, because there are different components of a press kit and you can choose to use some components and not others. This way you can customize the press kit depending on who you're sending it to.

Getting Past the Receptionist

Consider the receptionist like a gatekeeper who is there to keep people out, unless someone is expecting you or you can convince the receptionist you are expected, know the person you want to contact, or have something of interest, which he or she will want to know about.

To increase your chances of getting through by phone or to arrange a personal meeting, it helps to already know the name of the person you hope to see. Don't just ask for the editor of a particular topic. If you don't already know that person's name, find out.

For instance, if you look on most newspapers, it will have a page where they list all the people's names, e-mails, and phone numbers. Or turning your pitch into two calls – the first call to ask for the name of the right contact person and their preferred method of contact; the second call to ask for that person by name. The reason for this two step process is that if you have the person's name, you can call later and ask for that person by name. Preferably make the second call a day or two later, so if you speak to the same person on the whole, he or she doesn't realize you are the same person who just asked for the name of the person to call – a good way to get a quick brush and not get your call put through.

Sending an Initial Query by E-Mail

As an alternative to phoning or arranging for a personal meeting, send an e-mail. If you already have a business car or signup list with that person's e-mail, you're home free.

In some cases, you can find out an e-mail by seeing if the company uses a common format for each name, such as first initial, last name or full name, last initial at a particular company. Once you know what the formula is, you can put in the appropriate name or initials of that person in, and voila, you have a new contact for your e-mail database, and you can send an e-mail.

Using Your Media Contact's Preferences

While you may have your own preference for contacting the media to pitch a story – ie: initial phone call and follow-up e-mail; initial e-mail and follow-up phone call, it helps to know the preferences of the different media or the particular contact you want to reach. This way you can adapt your approach according.

For example, I found that the print media editors tend to prefer e-mails. At one time, they were big fans of the letter accompanied by an SASE (a self-addressed stamped envelope). But now almost everyone seems to prefer e-mails to initial phone calls, because when someone is writing something, phone calls can be disruptive. So it's better to send e-mails to most print media contacts, unless you are doing a follow-up call to see if they got your e-mail and hope to find out what else they may want from you (ie: to set up an interview, to get additional information, to get a press packet, etc.)

Tying Your Story to the Latest News

You are more likely to get your story covered if you can tie it in with what's in the news. So think of ways to make this tie-in. For instance, it may not matter that you have created what you think is a revolutionary new product. But if it's relevant and you can talk knowledgeably about that news event, that's a more compelling story.

For instance, say your product and service helps to keep track of people entering and leaving a building. You might mention how it might help the police identify inside crime suspects, such as in the Yale Murder case where a grad student working with mice was missing for five days and was found buried in a wall, after police determined she hadn't left the building.

Ideally, have an already written press release or letter which you can adapt to something in the news, so you can respond more quickly rather than writing up a new release or letter from scratch. You can easily adapt a prepared release, because you already have most of it written. Then you add in a few sentences to tie it in to something that's in the news now. For instance, if you have a product or method that might improve relationships, you might note how you might help resolve a conflict between a well-known celebrity couples that has recently hit the news.

The Power of Buzz and Referrals

While the assertive proactive and direct approach can get you press, sometimes you can effectively use an indirect approach, where you create buzz and get people to talk about you. Then, when the media hears about this interest, they will call you. You don't have to sell the media on doing the story; they are already interested.

As an example of the power of this indirect approach, I got two syndicated news stories that helped me expand a business where writers send out e-mail queries to the media with the help of special software. I didn't try to contact the media myself. Instead, in one case, I talked to people about the service at a number of business mixers, and people began talking about my business. This led to a reporter from the *Contra Costa Times* in the East Bay area calling me and doing an article on my company. In the second case, a former client who sold a book through the service told a *Wall Street Journal* reporter interviewing her about her book how she found an agent who sold her book through the service, and the reporter contacted me to do a story about how the service helped this writer and others. The result is the story ran in the *Wall Street Journal*. In both cases, within a few weeks, I had over 30 to 40 new clients – all because of a single article.

That's the ideal situation where you're doing some interesting things and a reporter or TV producer hears about you from somebody else. Then, they may feel even more excited about doing a story on you, because they can feel they discovered you and have an early exclusive on the story, so they want to feature it. By contrast, if the media contacts express interest in response to a query letter or press release, they may feel they are one of a number of media people following the story, so they are less excited about doing it.

Gaining Interest from Radio and TV Stations.

While the host is more visible on a radio or TV talk show, commonly the producer arranges for the interviews with the guests. The exception is when the host is also acting as a producer, which is most common on a small station. So often the host often does not make his or her own selections. Thus, to set up an interview, the person you want to contact is the producer, unless the same person is assuming both roles, whether you initially call or send a fax or e-mail.

Commonly, producers and hosts prefer to get the stories and guests pitched to them by e-mail. The same rules for follow-up as with print kick in if there is interest. You determine what they most want from you and in what format (ie: e-mail, fax, regular mail); then you send it and follow-up to set up the interview.

CHAPTER 3:
CREATING YOUR PRESS MATERIALS

CREATING A PRESS KIT AND PRESS RELEASE

When you first contact the media by e-mail or fax, initially send out a press release or query letter. Or if you first call, be ready to follow up with a release or a letter. Also, you will often want to have a press kit with more detailed information, such as questions an interviewer might ask you, bio information, a photo, catalog sheet, CD, or product sample.

Sending Out a Press Release or Query Letter

Sometimes you will send out the press releases or query letters first and then make a follow up call. In other cases, you will make the initial call and follow-up with a press release or query letter.

In either case, don't send your release or letter as an attachment. You might include a link to a website if you have one, but don't send an attachment with text, graphics, or photos. The reason to avoid doing this is that an attachment not only slows the e-mail down, but people are suspicious of getting viruses, trojans, spyware, and malware from unknown senders. In fact, some people will tell you "Don't send me anything unless you have my permission," and when they grant it, they will also tell you what format they want the material in (ie: Word, PDF, or other formatting).

Once people do ask for material from you, it's fine to send an attachment if they ask for the information this way. But it is still more impressive if you put the print-outs together into a binder, and some people prefer to receive any samples of your product, service, or writing that way. If you do put your material into a physical binding, you can mail or personally deliver it – and that personal touch can help increate interest in your project.

WHAT TO INCLUDE IN A PRESS RELEASE

A press release is normally 1 or at most 2 pages. Write it like a news article, featuring the who, what, where, when, and how elements in the first paragraph, so recipients can quickly know what the release is about.

A press release commonly includes these elements:

- headline and sometimes a subhead

- "for immediate release" line

- body copy

- contact information (put on the top in a regular mailed or faxed release; at the end in an e-mail release)

Headline or Subject Line

Your headline or subject line is critical. It entices recipients to want to read the rest of your release. Keep it short and catchy.

In a regular printed release, you might have a short ALL CAPS headline, followed by a longer Title Case subhead. But if you are sending an e-mail, unless you have a very long headline, put both in the subject line, which should be a maximum of 20-25 words, and ideally 10-15.

Make your headline very specific to what you're doing. Don't be vague or write a headline that reads like promotional or sales copy, such as "Exciting new event that will change America." Instead, write it like a headline for a news story, and if there's a tie-in to something in the news include that, such as: "New identity theft service helps police track down identity thieves; helped NYPD capture a killer."

If there is a dated event, include the date when that is happening on the headline, so you make it compelling for the recipient to open their e-mail right away.

You need to make your headline very clear, specific, and compelling, because many of the people in the media get hundreds and thousands of e-mails a day, and your headline or subject line can determine whether they open your e-mail or not.

If you're sending out a press release by e-mail, put the headline both in the subject line and in the body copy, because once the press release is printed out, it may not have the subject line on it.

Using a Subhead

Using a subhead is optional if your headline contains all the information you want to convey. Or use a subhead to clarify or explain your subject.

"For Immediate Release" Introduction

In an e-mail release, start off with a "For Immediate Release" line at the beginning of your press release before you repeat the headline and subhead in the body of your copy. In a printed release, it goes first before the headline and subhead

If the announcement is very time sensitive, such as for an event occurring in a day or two, include a date in the headline or subhead. But more typically, start with "for immediate release."

Writing Your Release Like a News Story

After your headline and any subhead, write your press release like a news story, where you begin with the what, when, where, why, and how in the first few sentences. The reason for doing this is you present the essence of the story first, which helps readers decide if they want to know more. Also, this approach enables any publication or media outlet picking up your story to cut from the bottom up if necessary, leaving the most important points of your story in the remaining text.

Using this news story approach also makes it possible for some publications, especially the smaller ones, can pick up your story as is, because they don't have the time and the staff to write their own articles, apart from a few assignments. In other cases, your release may inspire other editors and writers to write their own story, usually by contacting you for more information.

Contact Information

In a traditional release sent by regular mail or fax, the contact information should go in the top left or right hand corner. On e-mails, it is better to put this contact information in the end at the bottom left, because that way you get people right into the story when they look at it online.

The Difference Between a Press Release, Query Letter, and Social Media Posting

An alternate to writing a press release is to write up your information as a query letter. The main difference between the release and the letter is that a query letter is more personalized, though you can include the same information in both. Think of it this way. The press release goes out to many different people in the media, while a query letter is directed towards a particular person.

Sometimes, whether you are sending a release or a letter, you may have the name of the contact, sometimes you will only have the person's position or e-mail. Whatever the situation, write the letter as if it is going to a particular person, even though you don't address that person by name.

By contrast, when you send a press release, it is clear by the "for immediate release" that this release is not only going to that recipient, whether you include that person's name or not. Rather, it is being sent out to the media for publication or dissemination by whoever receives it.

You can also post much of the same information in a press release or query letter in an announcement posted in the social media, like LinkedIn or Facebook. In fact, some people even post press releases as is.

If you are charging for an event, it may not work well to send out a press release, because the media people will think of this as a commercial event, which you should advertise or list in an events calendar, rather than trying to get an article about it. The major exception is when an event features a big star, someone in the news, or is a benefit for a charity or high-profile victim. But for the run of the mill of event, there are so many events going on that a press release will generally be ignored.

Finding Contacts to Send Your Release or Query Letter

When you are doing local PR, you can build your media list by looking at the masthead of local publications or going online to get contact information for local radio or TV stations. To create your list of contacts, look for the editor or producer who handles your type of story, such as a business editor, entertainment editor, or features editor. Or call these media sources to ask for the names and e-mails of the appropriate media contact.

For large scale PR, you can either create your own database or use a service that can send your release or letter to hundreds or thousands of media contacts. Two of the services that do this are CornerBarPR and Cision.

CornerBarPR is a less expensive service with about 80,000 contacts in its database. They are organized by 17 major trade categories, such as business, health, and lifestyles/features, and by the different types of media (newspapers, magazines, radio, TV, wire services, and the online media). In addition, they are organized by local and national categories, so you can either pick up everyone in a particular media category or beat, or zero on contacts in a particular state or metropolitan area.

Cision is the largest of these services with a database of about 300,000 media contacts in the U.S., including newspapers, magazines, radio, TV, and now Internet media and blogs. You can target your contacts based on geographic area, type of media, beat, circulation. It costs about $3000 to $5,000 a year to have an account there, depending on the size of your organization, and a lot of publicists and big corporations have an account with them.

You can use these services to find particular contacts, as many publicists do. They selectively pick out people to contact and contact them individually. Or you can do a category or power search, where you select the type of media, beats, and other characteristics, and do a broad search, generating a large number of contacts. In Cision, you can find up to 5000 contacts in one search and export up to 2000 contacts in a .cvs or Excel file.

You can then do a bulk mailing, once you have your contact information in a .cvs or Excel format. There are a number of bulk mailing software programs you can buy, such as Group Mail, which I use for sending out mailings. Or you can use a service like the PR and Networking Connection (www.prandnetworkingconnection.com) or the News Media Connection (www.newsmediaconnection.com), to send out the mailing for you to the contacts obtained from a search of the database. Either way, whether you get your own software or use one of these services, the software can personalize your release or letter to go to the particular individuals at the selected media if this information available, or it can send your release or letter to whoever is at that particular e-mail.

CREATING A PRESS KIT

Generally, you use a press kit after you have gotten interest from a phone call, press release, or query letter and the media contact wants more information.

Typically, a press kit contains a selection of the following materials. While the starred items will almost always be included, you can choose the others as appropriate for your media contact.

- *your press release or query letter (even if you have sent this out, include it, as a summary and reminder of what your story is about).

- an optional cover letter than summarizes the story and introduces what's in the press kit

- *a one-sheet overview of your product, service, or you as a speaker

- *an individual or company bio

- a list of questions and answers

- one or more photos

- a CD or DVD

- testimonials sheet

- product samples

Increasingly, these press kits are sent via e-mail attachments or are featured on a Website. But many media people prefer the traditional kit to be sent to them by regular mail or given to them personally.

Selecting Items to Use in Your Press Kit

The advantage of having a variety of items to select from for your press kit is that you can choose what's appropriate to include for each contact. Some people will want just the basics – the press release and a one-sheet or bio for example, while others will want additional items, such as questions to ask and photos. By selectively deciding what to send and in what format, you not only cater to what the contact wants, which increases your chances of getting featured, but you cut down your time and costs by not sending unnecessary items.

For instance, if your press kit is going to the radio, besides the release and one sheet, you might have a list of questions that the host might ask you, such as: "How did you happen to develop this product or service? How did you make these connections to get this video produced?" A good way to create this list of questions is to note what questions people repeatedly ask you about your product or service, then put those down.

If you have photos, include the prints in a traditional media kit. Or if you send a photo by e-mail, send a jpeg.

Sometimes if appropriate, include a CD or DVD with photos, videos, product demos, songs, or testimonials in a traditional press kit. Or if you are e-mailing a press kit, include the information as attachments or include links to a Website with this information. Sometimes including product samples works well if you have a small, easy to mail product, and it's not expensive to include a sample. For example, I've sometimes gotten samples of books or pet products, such as pet food, jewelry and toys. Such samples can be a good way to increase interest in the product, since people can try them out and report on their experience – which hopefully be a good one.

If you can get testimonials, that can really help, particularly if these are from well-known people or people with a high status position, who have used and like your product or service. If you only have one or two testimonials, you might include them on the one-sheet overview of your product, service, or company. Or if you have a substantial number of testimonials, you might include a sheet of testimonials.

Whenever you list testimonials, put the most important ones first, either based on the person's name or title, or by the company where he or she works.

Types of Presentation Folders to Use

For a traditional press kit, use a folder with pockets on either side, so you can easily decide what items to include in your kit. These folders come in different colors and styles. A simple black or maroon folder offers a nice professional look, and a textured dark plastic cover looks good, too. Avoid bright reds, oranges, yellows, pinks, purples, and anything that glows or sparkles. Sure, they'll stand out, but not in a good way, unless you're are promoting some trendy, with-it item, like a rock band.

Sending Your Press Kit by E-Mail

If you are sending your press materials by e-mail, you can send separate attachments for each item. Or to make your material easier to review, combine everything together into a single attachment. The most common format now is the PDF, since anyone can read it on any type of computer.

If you have your documents in several PDF files, you can consolidate them into a single PDF, which many media people prefer because this keeps everything together. If you aren't sure, ask if your media contact wants everything in one attachment or separate attachments.

In either case, send any photographs in separate attachments, so they can be printed. Check on the resolution desired, too. The typical Website format is 72 dpi (which refers to the number of pixels per inch). But often if a photograph is going to be printed in a newspaper or magazine, a high resolution format is preferred, such as a 200 or 300 dpi format. Or the publication may even request a 300 dpi .tif file, which provides a much higher quality for reproduction than a JPEG.

<u>When to Send Out Your Material</u>

In sending out your material, as previously noted, it's best to begin with an initial phone call, e-mail, or personal meeting to quickly describe what you are promoting. Then, send out your press kit with the basics and any additional items appropriate for that contact. This way you cut down on your time and expenses of sending press kits to media contacts who aren't interested and will be likely to ignore or toss whatever you send.

When approaching media contacts by e-mail, don't send any attachments initially, because so many people are afraid of opening up e-mails that might have a virus, spyware, or malware. So they are likely to hit delete. Rather, get permission first, so the media contact is expecting what you send.

CHAPTER 4:
USING A WEBSITE OR BLOG
IN YOUR PR CAMPAIGN

An alternative or addition to sending a press kit is creating a Website and/or blog to promote your product or service. The site or blog can be another way to feature whatever you are promoting, plus you can direct media contacts to a page on the site from which they can download your press kit.

This approach works particularly well when the files of material in your press kit are too large to send by e-mail, and you want to quickly and inexpensively provide follow-up material, rather than printing and sending this material by regular mail.

USING A WEBSITE FOR PROMOTION

While a standard Website has a number of pages, consider getting a separate domain name for a promotional website, also known as a landing or squeeze page. Then, if you send out a press release or do a Google ad campaign, this is the Web page that you give out to go to for further information.

The reason for using a stand-alone page is that people may get distracted if they go to a website and there are other links to explore. By contrast, using a landing or squeeze page gets people to go where you want them to go. This stand-alone approach is often recommended by marketers for when you are selling a product or a service, because instead of buying something, the prospects might follow the links and leave your website and not come back. A similar strategy works well in doing PR. You direct the media contact to a single page that includes all of the information you want to provide about your story.

Using Search Engine Optimization and Keywords to Increase Website Traffic

A good way to get prospective customers and clients to your Website is using Search Engine Optimization or SEO techniques to get increased traffic to your site. This technique involves putting keywords throughout your website, so your site is more likely to turn up in the search engines.

You can obtain assistance in identifying what keywords to use through Google "Adwords" by doing a keyword search for your field. Google will indicate the most common words or phrases that people are using to search for your type of product or service and indicate how popular they are. Though Google is providing this information so you will select the keywords to bid on for your ad campaign, you can use this information to aid you in designing your site.

Then, after you identify the most popular words or phrases, incorporate them into the copy on your Website. Add the words or phrases if you aren't already using them or repeat them more often if you already have them on your site.

While you want to use popular keywords or phrases frequently on your site, integrate them into your copy, so they make sense. Don't just stock your Website with keywords that are not relevant to your product or service. Not only might you get a lot of visitors who won't be interested in what you are promoting, but you may risk getting banned from future searches for that Website if you are discovered. That's because you have misrepresented your Website and provided confusing information for the search engines.

If you have someone designing your Website for you, check if he or she is aware of SEO marketing and can incorporate these key words in the copy on the site. If not, find someone to write the copy who is familiar with the process, or write the copy yourself with the appropriate key words.

Using Your City to Target Your Market

A good way to start with SEO is to seek local interest in your product or service first, since you will have less competition for rankings than if you are seeking a high ranking nationally, where you are competing with people all over the U.S.

To obtain this local interest, put the name of your city in your copy from time to time, so you will come up in a higher position in your own market area. For example, an attorney in Houston, Texas might mention on his home page the different types of legal work that he does several times by placing them in different sentences. This way, he has integrated this information in his copy and is not just repeating this information in a series of lists, which might be identified as spam. Also, he might mention that he is located in Houston in several sentences, thereby increasing the chances that a search for attorneys in Houston will bring up his name.

Using Flash on Your Website

While many people like Flash for its dramatic effects, it's not a good idea to use it on your website, because it distracts from search engine optimization. That's because Google and the other search engine don't have a way to crawl Flash with their search engine spiders. Then, too, many people will skip the Flash opening and go directly from the opening page to the rest of your site. So using Flash is often a waste of time and money, as well as not being good for SEO, though an exception is when you have something very visual to present. For example, some industries use a lot of Flash pages to provide that extra pizzazz, such as the movie industry for promoting videos and music.

But generally, it is better not to have Flash dominate your home page, because it interferes with optimization and in many industries, people don't pay much attention to it. Perhaps have a small Flash section for dramatic flair, but create most of the Website in html, which is the main coding format that the search engines recognize.

WRITING A BLOG

Besides posting your PR release on your website, you can write it as an article on your blog. Or you can write an original article and attract interest to that.

Having a blog on your Website is a good idea, since it contributes to search engine optimization if you keep it updated. Generally two or three times a week is ideal. The advantage of having a blog and doing these updates is that the search engines are continually searching out new information, so when you update the blog, the search engine picks that up, contributing to a higher ranking for your Website. So more people are likely to find your site if you have a blog on your site, rather than using a stand-alone blog, such as on WordPress or blogger, with a link to your site.

Thus, while you can readily set up a blog on popular blogging sites like WordPress or www.blogspot.com, it's a good idea to tie your blog to your Website, such as by setting up Word Press on your site and creating a link, such as www.yourdomain/blog, that goes to WordPress.

In addition, once people find your blog, anyone reading it can immediately go to your Website to explore and learn more about you and your products and services. (They just have to eliminate the /blog from your URL and they are there). You can also include a link in your blog to a page where you feature your books, products or services, so those who are interested will go directly to that webpage to learn more and even buy online.

Turning Your Blog Into an Article

You can get even more mileage from a blog by turning it into an article. You can post your article for free on ezines.com, which will include up to two links in your article to your Website or wherever else you want to link. Then, when people read your articles, they may go to your website or to a special PR page you have designated.

Pitching Your Article to the Print Media

You might also pitch your article from a blog – or any article -- to the print media to increase your visibility. You will get much more response from the media if you offer your article for free, which is normally what you want to do when you do PR. When you use the articles for promotion, you are less interested in getting paid for an article – and normally you'll only get a small amount anyway, say up to $150 for an exclusive for a designated period.

If you do use the article on different places, rewrite it slightly so it looks like a new article. Otherwise Google and the other search engines may only pick up the first article, because they think of the other article as a duplicate, which it is. So the search engines won't pick it up again.

Turning Blogs from Articles to E-Books and POD Books

Besides writing a blog to promote an e-book or turning it into an article, when you get a number of articles, you can turn them into another e-book. Then you can turn any kind of e-book into a print-on-demand book. So these various types of writing blend together, and you can easily go from one to another, including turning an e-book into a series of articles and a blog or turning articles and blogs into e-books and print-on-demand books.

For example, I wrote a book called 17 TOP SECRETS TO KEEP YOUR JOB OR FIND NEW WORK, which started off with my publisher coming to me and saying: "We'd like you to do some articles so people are aware of your WANT IT, SEE IT GET IT! book. So I started writing articles about how to apply these techniques, and what everybody wanted to know about was: "How do you keep a job if you hate your boss?...How do you get a new job while you currently have a job you don't like?" and other job keeping or finding topics. So I ended up writing about a dozen articles about that and later turned these into blogs. Eventually, I collected them together to create an e-book, and then I turned that into a print-on-demand book through ASJA Press.

Later, I found ways to publishing this same book in other formats, such as CreateSource, which creates both an e-book available for download and a print-on-demand book. After you send in your ready to bind Word document, you select a cover template and indicate what text and photo you want to use. Then, the company sends you a proof, and your only upfront cost is for that – about $4-5, plus $6 for shipping. Once you approve the proof, you can order as many books as you want to sell yourself, and the company pays you a percentage on what they sell – about 60%.

Frequency, Length, and Format for a Blog

Ideally, blog two to three times a week or even daily, because search engines are continually seeking new information; so each time you write a new blog they will pick that up.

Blogs tend to be a little shorter than any articles, but you can combine a couple blogs together to create a larger article. Or write a longer blog that can be published as an article. Commonly, blogs are about 300-400 words; articles for newspapers about 600-800 words and for magazines about 800-1500 words.

I have set up a blog to be easily published as an article by putting a headline on each blog in addition to the usual date of writing it, which is like having an article on my blog. Then I have combined a series of articles into both an e-book and print-on-demand book. Or conversely, you can copy and paste articles you have written into a blog.

Common formats for writing your blog are WordPress and Blogger. While you can simply write a blog on a page on your Website, these software programs add additional functionality, such as including your blog in RSS feeds and adding your blog to your LinkedIn profile.

You can create a stand alone blog in which you open up a WordPress account or Blogger account, which is like having a blog on a platform hosted by Word Press or Blogger. Some of these blogs are free, though you can get premium upgrades on them, such as to get extra storage or be able to add video to your blog.

Rather than writing a stand-alone blog, if you have a website, it's a good idea to put Word Press on your own website, such as I have done at <u>www.ginigrahamscott.com/blog</u>. The advantage of doing it this is that when people see your blog, they can easily go to your website. So your blog helps to draw traffic to your website.

CHAPTER 5:
SENDING YOUR PRESS
MATERIALS TO THE
MEDIA

How do you get your press release out to the media? Here are some ways to build a list or use a PR release service.

PR Release And Posting Services

There are services like PR Newswire or BusinessWire, which provide a newswire service that some publications subscribe to or they send out a release with a series of articles, like the old ticker tapes used to do. Some of these services are fairly expensive however, with the costs around $200 for limited distribution to particular markets, and several thousand for a more comprehensive distribution. And the costs are even higher when you add in photos and video packages.

Another service is PR Web, where you can opt for various levels of service from $80 to $360 for each press release. The basic service gets your release featured on PR Web and on top sites, like Yahoo and Google. An expanded service gets you social media visibility. The top service gets your release distributed through the Associated Press and directly to top newspapers.

A less expensive PR release service is the PR and Networking Connection, an offshoot of NewsMediaConnection.com, a business which I sold but am still associated with. The service has seven different media categories, including daily and community newspapers, newswires and syndicates, radio and talk show hosts, radio stations, magazines, TV, and Online media. Prices start at $250 for any one media, $350 for two, $450 for three, and then there's a sliding scale with $800 for all seven.

Still another service is Expertclick, which costs about $700 to $900 a year, depending on when you sign up. Using the service, you can post a series of press releases, up to once a week, and journalists come to their website. I used them for several years, though I didn't get much response. They work for some people, but not for everybody.

Finally, you will find some Websites where you can post releases for free, though they aren't that effective, since they depend on the media coming to the site. But the media already gets blasted with so many e-mails each day that they don't need to search for releases; a huge number of releases already come to them.

PR DATABASE SERVICES

There are also some PR databases which you can use if you send out your own releases. One of the less expensive service which I have used is CornerBarPR at www.cornerbarpr.com, which has two services – the full service for about $700 a year, which allows you to export data and create your own customized media lists. It has about 80,000 contacts in its database and covers the most popular beats, including Arts/Entertainment, Computers/High-Tech, Food/Beverage, General Science/Technology, Health/Fitness/Medicine, Investment/Banking/Financial Services, Lifestyle/Features, andTravel/Hospitality.

Another service that has a much more extensive database, which the major PR agencies and large corporations use, is Cision.com, which offers a "Cision Point" service for searching the media. You can do a search of the database by type of media, geographic location, beat, audience size, and other factors, and can export up to 2000 entries into a .csv or Excel file. Plus you can do special searches for individuals contacts in the media, such as if you want to contact someone on Oprah. But it's a fairly expensive service at about $3000 a year for an individual or small company; $5000-60000 for larger companies with multiple users.

DOING YOUR OWN E-MAIL BLAST

If you want to send out your own releases or query letters, you can get a special software that enables you to send out personalized releases to the contacts in your database, and send them out from and get replies to whatever e-mail you want to use. It's a program I've used for over six years, and it's great for such mailings.

It's called Group Mail and you can get it from infacta.com for about $400 to sign up, and yearly updates are about $60 a year. You put in whatever e-mail you want to use in the send and reply fields. This way you can easily use a special e-mail for your PR campaign to keep track of the responses you get. Using individual mailings for different campaigns is a good idea, much like putting codes on direct mail pieces, so you can assess which mailings are the most effective.

In doing these e-mail blasts, be prepared for about an 8% return rate, even if you are using recently updated data, because there is so much mobility in the media. That's why it's good to set up a special e-mail for the mailing, particularly since if you do a very large mailing, this high rate of return could trigger your e-mail provider to shut down your service, which is most likely if you use a free account, such as Yahoo. For example, if you send out 20,000 e-mails, you would get about 1500 back with an 8% return rate.

If you plan to sending out a large e-mail blast, try staggering your mailing over two or three days to reduce the chances of triggering a filter that deems a large number of returns in a limited time period to be a sign of spam, which could lead to a shut down. Generally, such a shut down will take about 24 hours to occur, and since most media contacts will respond within the first day, if you monitor your e-mail closely after sending out a mailing, you won't lose any valuable contacts who want more information (and you can always switch to another e-mail to respond to them).

CHAPTER 6:
THE IMPORTANCE OF
FOLLOW-UP

An important part of PR is developing on ongoing relationship with people in the media. You can start doing this when you do your first PR campaign and get to know people when you follow-up. Then, as you continue to do PR, you will gain an increasing advantage as you contact the same media people again and again, assuming you have had a series of favorable contacts.

MAKING FAVORABLE CONTACTS

Developing these positive contacts comes from being respectful and not too pushy, and providing useful information that makes a good story when you send e-mails or faxes or call. You need to be diplomatic in building a good relationship over time, which means picking up cues about what the person is interested in and following through as promised after a contact. Otherwise, you can burn your bridges, making it more difficult to contact that media person in the future.

Whether this is your first contact or a subsequent one, follow up is critical. You may get some results from an initial press release or query letter mailing. But often it helps to follow up with a phone call to make sure the contact received the e-mail (if not, send another) and to check if he or she might be interested in doing a story. Because media people get so many e-mails, often a good story could be lost in the clutter. So sometimes your brief call may be all the contact needs to realize that this would be an interesting story to do.

PR RELEASE FOLLOW UPS

Thus, after you send out your press release or query letter, a good way to follow up is with a phone call to make sure people got the information you sent or see if they want additional information. It's a good idea to wait two or three days after you send the release to see if they will respond; then if you don't hear from them, follow-up with the phone call. If they say they didn't get it – which may be because media people get a high volume of e-mails and faxes – send it again.

Should you get a voice mail, try calling back later to attempt to contact the person directly, rather than leaving a message. But if you get a voice mail each time you call, leave your message. If you get an assistant or receptionist, try to get through to the media contact directly, possibly by asking for another time when you can call. But if you don't get through after a couple of times or the assistant or receptionist seems resistant, leave your message. You've done your best, and you don't want to seem like an insistent pest.

This kind of follow-up can become quite tedious when you have many people to call, because you are asking the same questions over and over. So this can be a good time to use an assistant or surrogate posing as you to follow up.

Another approach after you've done a mass e-mailing is to follow-up with an updated e-mail to those who haven't responded. In this case, you send much the same information, but you change the headline and rewrite it slightly, so it looks like you are sending something new. For example, say 20 people have contacted you after a mailing or after some initial phoning. You don't want to insult their intelligence by sending a follow-up letter with the original information to them, since they have already responded. Instead, when you do the mass e-mailing to everybody in your database, exclude those people who responded already.

Commonly, if the media people decide early on they aren't interested in your story, they will discard your material right away. Or if they are possibly interested, they will put it in a file for possible stories. But after a certain period, if they haven't used it, they will ditch it, and after awhile, they may not even remember you have sent your material. In fact, I wouldn't trust somebody putting something in a file and finding it a month or two later. So after this amount of time, you can freely send that media contact similar information again.

CHAPTER 7:
TIMING YOUR PRESS
CAMPAIGN

Different media work on different time schedules, so time your campaign around the lead times needed to increase your chances of getting coverage.

Internet

The timeline for the Internet is often instantaneous when you send out your information through the social media liked LinkIn or Twitter or to the Internet media. If the media contact is interested, the information can appear right away in print or you may get a quick response to set up an interview.

Newspapers

Newspapers also tend to have a short time-line – a few days for a daily paper; a few days to a week for a community newspaper. Typically, with a daily paper, send your information about a week or ten days in advance and follow up a few days before the event. If it's a weekly paper, send your information about two weeks in advance and follow up ten days in advance.

Radio

With radio, lead times can vary. With some programs, you may get booked in a day or two, and sometimes a host or producer may call asking you to go on right away. In other cases, a host or producer may book a show several weeks in advance. Usually, you will do a call-in interview from the comfort of your home or office.

TV

With TV, times can vary, too – commonly from a week to a few weeks. While sometimes a local news team may come to your location, often you will be asked to go to a studio in a major city, such as New York, L.A., or San Francisco, to record a video link up from there. If you live near that city, you're in luck. Otherwise, you have to travel to where the program is produced.

Sometimes a major program will pay for your travel expenses, such as for airfare, shuttle services, and parking. But commonly, especially in these recessionary times, you are expected to get to the studio on your own. So if you aren't able to travel to a distant location where a program is recorded, don't include any stations or shows in that area in your pitches for TV coverage.

Magazines

The longest lead time is commonly for magazines which come out monthly or less frequently. Often articles are planned two or three months out, sometimes even longer. So if you are looking for quick coverage, skip contacting magazines.

Calendar Announcements

If you are sending an announcement for a calendar event, allow plenty of time to get your announcement in before the deadline for that calendar. Generally, for these short items, there is no need to follow-up, and media people generally don't want you to do so, because they would be overwhelmed by a huge number of calls from all of their listings. So just send off any calendar items and hope for the best.

CHAPTER 8:
KEEPING TRACK OF
YOUR PR

WHEN TO EXPECT YOUR STORY TO APPEAR

It's nice to know when information about you will appear, whether it's in an article that includes you, an article you've written, or an interview with you.

Sometimes, the media contact will tell you, and occasionally will send you clips or links to an online interview. Though such alerts are more common with magazines. Often the best you can do is finding out the link to the publication and a date when the article with you or by you will appear.

But if possible, ask your media contact to send you a clip page or link or magazine, and sometimes the media contact will. Or if this is a future issue, ask when that will be online or on the stands, so you can check it out and obtain a copy.

To keep track of what is appearing when and what to do to get a copy, keep a tickler file to remind you that a particular feature is suppose to appear or an interview is supposed to air at such and such time. Check a few days in advance to see if it will still appear then. Sometimes schedules change, so by checking, you can be alert if it will appear on a different date.

TRACKING THE PR YOU SEND AND THE PUBLICITY YOU GET

It's a good idea to keep track of these media publications and appearances, because you can put the press you get on your Website or in a folder or binder for past press, which you can later add to your press kit. Then, that previous coverage can help you build even more coverage, as other media contacts see a growing interest about you in the media.

Sometimes other media will pick up the press you have already gotten from other news sources, such as articles that are distributed through the wire services or posted on various news sites on the Internet. But baring that, another way to use past PR to get more PR is to create a list or one-sheet of all the places where you have gotten stories. Then, include a few of the biggest features in your PR release or include a separate page listing the publicity you have gotten from what outlets and when in your press kit.

In both cases, you can use this past PR as leverage to get even more interest. For instance, say three dozen publications picked up your story in the last couple of weeks. Use that information in your press kit or press release, which you send to the larger media to show how your story has been picked up by these different places. Ask if they would be interested in doing a special story based on this. The larger media may not want to do exactly the same story but may want to write a story with their own take on it, which is ideal.

Also, keep a record of the releases you write and to whom you send what information to, so you don't send out the same releases again. If you are selectively contacting the media, note the specific media you have contacted. Or if you are sending a mass release to different types of media, keep track of which databases you have used to send your releases to different groups. Then, note the media contacts who have responded to you directly, so you can exclude them from future mass mailings.

CHAPTER 9:
GETTING YOUR WORK PUBLISHED

WRITING ARTICLES FOR PUBLICATION

Writing articles can increase your credibility in the field. And sometimes you can get paid for your articles to.

Deciding Whether to Offer Articles for Free or Pay

If you can offer free articles to the print media, you're more likely to get them published.

I have worked with some clients who wanted to get paid for their articles, and you can be paid if you have a unique article. However, the pay is commonly not very much – perhaps $150 to $500 for an exclusive for a certain period of time, and the lower amount is more common.

So consider whether you would rather write an article and get paid or use the article to gain more publicity for your product or service. Generally, it's worth more to offer the article for free and get it more widely published, along with your bio and link to your Website, than to get paid for a single article. Though possibly you may be able to do both by having one article you offer for payment and another article using the same or similar material which you offer for free. Just be sure they have different titles and are written and organized differently, so it doesn't look like you have plagiarized yourself.

Using an Article for Promotional Purposes

If you're mainly using the article for promotional purposes, offer it for free. I've gotten between 50-100 pick-ups in doing mass mailings to the media, and many of these publications told me where the article was going to appear.

Look at the offer to publish for free like an exchange. Typically, the magazine or newspaper publisher will print the free article in return for putting in a bio about you at the end and a link to your Website.

But whether you seek to publish for pay or for free, you can't sell a salesy kind of article. That's what you might write for an ad. Rather, the article has to be informative for readers, not just a promotional piece. For example, if you are interested in promoting Spanish wines, you might write something about trends in the wine industry or how to choose the right wines to go with a meal. Your article should be about trends or how-to in general, rather than about your particular product or service.

Typical Payment for Articles

As long as an article doesn't read like a commercial but offers a story of interest or provides valuable how-to tips, you can get paid. For example, one client offered an exclusive for a certain period of time and sold her article for $150, with the understanding that she would be free to publishing it elsewhere after three months.

You can similarly offer an exclusive for a limited period, and even for certain regions if you are pitching a regional publication that mainly has readers in that region. Then, after that time period is over, you can make the article available to others, though once it's published, other publications will be less open to paying or may want to pay less.

What you might get for an article depends on the type of media, circulation of the publication,   the length of your article, and if it is being published as an exclusive or not.

Magazines commonly offer more than newspapers. At one time, a typical payment was $1-2 a word for articles in the major magazines – or about $500-1000 for a 500 word article; about half of that in the trades. But now magazine payments are down because of the recession and the growing number of writers writing articles for free. For example, one client who sent out a query to magazines got offers from $100-200 for an 800 word article, though some magazines might offer $400-500 for an article of about the same length.

The payments by newspapers are generally much less, particularly since many newspapers are collapsing or reducing page lengths today. The payment is even less if it is a syndicated article, which is offered to multiple publications, though sometimes syndication agreements will provide that only one publication in a particular geographic area can publish the article. Typically, you can expect about $10-25 per article for these, so you depend on volume to make any money on such articles.

If you are doing self-syndication, you need to make these arrangements yourself and enter into agreements with each publication individually. Create your own agreement specifying how many articles are being purchased, how much for each one, and when you need to get additional articles to that publication.

Or if you are doing a series of articles or a regular column, an alternative to pitching the articles yourself and handling financial arrangements with each paper, is to pitch your article to a syndicate, which will send out the articles for you, usually on a 50-50 basis. However, it has become much more competitive to find a syndicate to do this, because of the cut-backs in the newspaper industry, since many newspapers are consolidating or going out of business. So now the syndicates are much less likely to take on new clients; they have enough trouble to continue to sell the articles of the clients they already have, though they may take on an occasional new client with a high-profile platform, such as a best-selling author or an expert in the news. If you can find a syndicate to represent you, great! But it's not very likely these days.

Thus, I recommend doing your own self-syndication and offer your articles for free. There is relatively little money in selling articles, and even if you do make a few sales, it can take a lot of time to manage the agreements and payments. So if you're priority is getting promotion for a product or service, it may not pay to try to get money from the article.

In fact, as soon as you say you're asking for money for an article, you won't hear from the media contact again. For instance, when I offered one article for free, I got about 40 pick-ups for it, including some Internet media and Websites that agreed to publish my articles in return for a bio and promotional links. By contrast, when I offered a series of columns, where the publisher could publish the first three columns for free and then I wanted payment, I only got 5 responses, and one publishers only published the first three articles, but nothing after that. In another case, the publisher said she would like to publish one of my series of 10 articles each week. But once I said the first three are free and asked "What's your budget?" for the rest, I never heard from her again. I even sent her two follow-up e-mails but she didn't answer.

So once you start talking about money, you'll get fewer people who will want to publish anything. The editors will pay the people on staff, but they don't have budget for outside people.

Using a PR Release to Offer Your Articles for Publication

As an alternative to writing a query letter inviting editors to publish your articles for free or for terms to be arranged, you can also send out a press release that invites editors to publish them, as long as you are offering them for no charge. It's a more formal way of inviting publication as well as letting editors know you are making this offer generally available. It's an ideal approach to use when your article is tied to something in the news and you'd like it published quickly, since commonly a press release means there is no need to respond and work out publication arrangements with you. The editor can simply go ahead and reprint article featured in the release.

Also, this approach can be used if you have a whole series of articles. Simply indicate that you have this series on a particular topics, and include the first article in the series with a list of other articles that are available. Then, if they like that article, they will ask you for more.

PUBLISHING YOUR ARTICLES ON EZINES

Ezines is a website where you can post articles in return for bio information and links to one or two Websites of your choice. And readers are welcome to post a link back to your article from another site. The listing contributes to your credibility, since people can read your articles and go to your website. And you can later post your release on your website, too. So it's a good place for creating awareness if you're not concerned with getting paid for your articles, since once you post an article here, it will be hard to sell it anywhere else.

The length of a article is typically about 500-700 words, sometimes up to about 1000-1500 words.

The site has proved to be very popular with writers, since there are about 200,000 authors who have posted articles on Ezines, and more and more writers join everyday. I have about a dozen articles there, and many other writers average about 10-15 articles, though some have many more, even hundreds or thousands.

The way to get your article listed is to simply send it in, indicating what category in which you want to place your article. The Ezines staffers will screen your article to see that it conforms to their guidelines and if it's not duplication of anything that they have. Then, if it is approved, they will post it on the site.

According to their guidelines, an article can't be only a commercial for your product or service, and you can't include more than two links to your own Websites or products. It has to be an informative article that people will find of interest other than just knowing about your events. For instance, if you're doing classes on yoga, rather than talking about your classes, you might talk about how the yoga movement is changing America, how yoga is beneficial to one's health, or some other topic of general interest about yoga. Then, you can include a short bio with information about your product or service at the end of the article, along with one or two links to your Website or product. Should the article need some changes to pass the review, the Ezines staff will tell you what is wrong, and after you edit it, they'll review it again and if it passes, finally list it.

While it is more typical to use these articles to promote yourself or products and services, you can also excerpt and adapt articles from a book to promote that book. Or you can collect these articles into books, as I have done, and then sell those.

For example, I wrote a series of articles as a result of requests from magazine and newspaper editor for tips on how to keep a job or find work based on my WANT IT, SEE IT, GET IT get it book. Though the editors just wanted a half-dozen or so tips, I turned them into my own articles which

I posted on Ezines. Then, after I had written a dozen articles on a similar theme, I collected them together, added a few more articles, and turned them into a book which is now for sale: 17 TOP SECRETS FOR HOW TO KEEP YOUR JOB OR FIND NEW WORK.

After your article is posted, you can later find out how many people have viewed your article. E-zines lists the articles in the order of the articles with the most interest, and they also have a graph that shows the number of views for each article. For instance, I've have about 2000 responses for all of my articles, and "Networking for the Newly Employed", the most popular article has 350 readers, "How to Find a Job" has 300 people. You don't get any personal information about the people viewing your articles, though if people read your article and want to know more about you, they can follow your links to your website and contact you directly from there.

CHAPTER 10:
USING E-BOOKS TO PROMOTE YOUR PRODUCT OR SERVICE

THE IMPORTANCE OF E-BOOKS

E-books have become an important marketing tool, because you can use an e-book to create more awareness for yourself and increase your credibility. That's because having an e-book shows your expertise in your field, whether a person buys your e-book or not. Then, too, an e-book can be a good promotional vehicle for your products or services, since people reading or learning about your e-book are likely to feel you're competent or your product will be good. Plus you can earn money from your books.

One common way e-books are published is in a PDF format. Then a buyer can download a book from a secure site after paying for it. Or to use these e-books as a free promotional perk, give customers, clients, or prospects the Website URL to download the book.

Another common form of publication is for an e-book reader, such as Kindle or for other types of readers, including on mobile devices.

You can go from E-books to print on-demand (POD) books very easily. For instance, if you are doing back-of-the room sales to sell your books at an event, you can bring a few samples for sale and take orders for the rest. Then, you can quickly and inexpensively turn an e-book into a printed book which looks like it has been commercially produced. The main difference is that the POD publisher prints and binds copies of the book in response to orders and can ship them to you or to the customer.

COPYRIGHT PROTECTION

Since an e-book in a PDF format is typically e-mailed to buyers or customers download it from a website, people commonly ask about copyright protection and if pirates are going to steal it. Usually the people buying your book won't do that; they are buying a single copy for themselves, not to distribute to others. Though if you register the copyright, you can go after any serious infringers should this problem occur.

You have automatic copyright on the book, granted under the Bern Convention. Also, you can register the copyright with the U.S. Copyright Office for added protection, since you can get statutory damages – about $100,000 and legal fees for each violation. By contrast, if something isn't registered, you can only get actual damages, which can be minimal or hard to prove. Forget trying to use what's commonly called the Poor Man's Copyright, where you send a copy of your book or other items to be copyrighted to yourself and don't open the envelope. That strategy doesn't work, since anyone can open the envelope at any time and put something in the envelope. You still have an unregistered copyright.

However, even if you register a copyright, you can't monitor small scale individual copying very easily. And usually the main problem with copying is with music, not typically books. The best protection is to put a warning on the book indicating that all rights are reserved and no one may copy any part of the book without written permission. Then, if anybody does copy and distribute your book on a massive scale and you find out about this, with a registered copyright, you can pursue statutory damages. But in practice, people can readily copy your material informally without you knowing it and any copyright litigation is very expensive, so it is not realistic to pursue most copyright infringements. Besides, a primary purpose in publishing an e-book is to get publicity and increase your credibility for marketing your product or service. Usually the income from the book is only an added perk, but not the major source of income in publishing the book. That comes through getting more clients and sales.

MARKETING AND DISTRIBUTING YOUR E-BOOK

Selling an E-Book in a PDF Format

One popular way of marketing and distributing an e-book is by setting up a landing page, also called a "squeeze page," where you feature the benefits of your e-book. It's called a landing or squeeze page, because that's where you send people with your ads.

The page should include an auto-responder where you collect e-mail addresses and a series of buy buttons, interspersed with the copy, so people can buy online. Begin with a powerful headline that captures the interest of the reader, followed by copy and a photo or video touting the many benefits people will get from the product or service. Then, include the first of several buy buttons followed by more copy and another buy button. A typical landing page features several of these sections with alternating content and buy buttons. The content is written to draw the prospect on, while the buy buttons give the prospect repeated opportunities to buy.

Then, if a person wants to buy and clicks a buy button, he can place his order on line and pay through PayPal, Amazon payments, or a credit card. Once the buyer pays, he is taken to another page where he can download the e-book. An alternate way is for you to get the order, and then you manually send a thank-you and e-mail the e-book.

I've sold e-books as PDFs in both ways. I sold about 200 e-books on "Sell Your Book, Script, or Column", when I owned the PublishersAndAgents business, primarily for promotional purposes. When someone ordered the book, the cost was $10 via PayPal or a Credit Card. I manually sent them a link to download the book, and to add some protection, I saved each copy with a password made up of their first name and the initial of their last name. Then, if they placed an order for sending out a query within a week, they could apply their $10 e-book purchase to the cost of a query, which cost $240-380. While about 200 people ordered the book, 25 of them subsequently ordered the query services. So what I really wanted in offering the e-book was to convince people to order the service, which about 10% of the people ordering the book did.

Selling Your E-Book through an Online Reader

An increasingly popular way to sell e-books now is through an e-book reader, such as the Kindle. There are about a dozen popular reader formats now, and you can generally upload and convert the book into that format from Word.

There are also some e-book publishers who act as intermediaries, where they format your book for these other readers, such as SmashWords. However, you have to set up a Word document according to their special guidelines, which include taking out tables and especially large headlines, which you might have set up for the PDF-format e-book.

PUBLISHING YOUR E-BOOK AS A PRINT-ON DEMAND BOOK

You can readily convert an e-book into a POD format with a number of companies. This way you have a physical book. I have worked with iUniverse on over 20 books, since I like the way the company does the formatting for you, whereas many other companies want you to format the book exactly as you want it published. Also, since I have a special arrangement as a member of rate of only $100 per book – or at no charge if I have a previously published book which is no longer in print. I can also provide that price to my ghostwriting clients, as long as my name is on the cover, such as "with" or "and" Gini Graham Scott. Otherwise, they would be treated like any other customer.

Some of the other well-known POD companies include LuLu, BookSurge, a division of AMAZON, Lightning Books, CreateSpace, and Trafford Publishing. Some of these companies have a set up charge, from about $100-500; others work on a royalty basis if you have your book already set up and ready to go. You can contact these different companies to obtain information on the cost and pricing of your book. Commonly the price depends on the number of pages, with an extra charge for interior graphics and photos, if you have any. Generally, these companies will provide you with a choice of photos and graphics for the cover, and in some cases, they have a design staff that will design the cover for you, subject to your approval.

THE FORMAT FOR AN E-BOOK

The typical format for an e-book is about 50-75 pages, which is shorter than a typical paperback or hardcover published book, which is about 250-300 pages or 100-150 pages for a shorter quick read book.

So if you've already written or published a longer book, you can easily divide it into smaller sections and make each one a different e-book. These sections than can become stand alone books or part of a series. Then, you can set a price for getting a single book in the series or the complete series, and generally your price for the whole set shouldn't be more than buying a hard-copy of the books, and the price for individual books should be even less – usually set so if you buy three or more books, the price is the same as getting all of them – an incentive to get the complete book.

For example, I did that with three of my books published by iUniverse, after I got back the rights from another publisher and turned each book into a series of e-books. I turned COLLECT THE MONEY PEOPLE OWE YOU, a 200 page book, into three books featuring the three stages of collecting money from protecting yourself against bad debts to persuading the person to pay to how you get tough with the debtor. I turned LET'S HAVE A SALES PARTY, a 350 page book, into seven books; the first is how to set up a party plan business, while subsequent books deal with how to find contacts, put on a great party, sell at the party, and follow-up after the party.

CHARGING FOR E-BOOKS

The way to price e-books depends on the value of what you are giving in your book and whether it's available at a regularly published book anyplace else.

If your book is already published, such as through iUniverse or a self-published POD book and the book is available on Amazon, you can't charge more than for the books somebody can get elsewhere. For example, I have three e-books in which I have divided up a larger POD book into several e-books of 40 to 70 pages each. I have charged $10 for each e-book, with a group rate for ordering all of them, but that rate is no larger than the cost of purchasing the book at Amazon. LET'S HAVE A SALES PARTY, for instance, sells for $29.95 through AMAZON, and is divided up into seven sections for $10 each. But all seven sections are $29.95 – the same as the POD book on AMAZON, though the advantage is the customer has no sales tax and shipping, and the book can be downloaded right away.

By contrast, you can charge substantially more of an e-book if you are offering special information not available anywhere else, which some people do. Say your book is about financial tips on how to save money on your mortgage. If the information is not generally available information, and the book is by a mortgage broker, the author could charge $30 to $40, because then the customer isn't just buying a book. Obtaining this information is more like getting a private consultation with an expert and getting highly valued knowledge that will provide great savings.

Another example of this special interest pricing is the people doing Internet marketing who are selling their e-books for $40-70. They are claiming to have special information and are making it seem very valuable, so they can sell it for more. And they may be able to turn these books into even more income, because often these e-books are a lead-in for more advanced information offered through expensive webinars and teleseminars, priced at several hundred dollars or more.

For instance, Jim Edwards has a series of books on writing and selling e-books, such as 30 DAYS TO WRITING AND PUBLISHING YOUR E-BOOK, priced at $29. Also, he has a package on consulting pitched to those who express interest in any of his e-books. Sometimes he will offer the initial teleseminar or webinar for free, since these are used as a promotional vehicle to get people to sign up for a more advanced program or series of classes. I experienced this when I participated in one of Edward's free teleseminars. About 2000 people were on the call, with people signing in from all over the world, because Jim was able to create and publicize a niche for himself as an Internet marketing and e-book guru. A few dozen other people in this field can similarly command top dollar for their books and seminars.

Some of the fields where you can charge top dollar include programs on using the social media to increase Web traffic and making money through Internet marketing. But don't expect to be able to immediately obtain such earnings, since the people charging these high fees are able to do so, because they have built a following and have gained credibility through the many different programs they offer.

It can take some time for you to build up what you can charge to that high level. Thus, you might start with a lower price to build sales initially. Then as you get testimonials from satisfied customers, start to charge more. You can also increase your charges as you build up more products to sell, such as by having videos and CDs of your programs, as well as an e-book.

A key to building up to high e-book earnings is to find a niche where you are offering unique information based on your area of expertise. For instance, some people in the film industry do this by creating programs on how to produce a film or sell your idea to TV, and they have put together a combination of e-books and CDs they sell for $300-400 a set. And as an incentive to buy, they position the package as a recording or material from a much more expensive $1000 to $1500 workshop – but now customers can get this material for only a few hundred dollars if they react right away before the offer is withdrawn..

WAYS TO PUT YOUR E-BOOK TOGETHER

The can put your e-book together in a number of ways or work with a ghostwriter to write it for you. These methods include the following:

- **From Notes**. Quickly write down what you want to include in your book. Don't try to polish up your notes. Just quickly jot down your ideas. Later you can select, organize, and edit them.

- **From Workshops and Seminars**. If you put on a program, tape it. Then, transcribe it yourself or hire someone to do this. Afterwards, select, organize, and edit this material.

- **From Interviews**. You can participate in these interviews over the phone or in person. Choose a good interviewer who can guide the questions. Possibly give the interviewer some questions you want to answer to start the process. Or let the interviewer develop the questions from your overview of the book.

- **From Talking to Yourself**. Talking to yourself is like conducting a self-interview. Create an outline for yourself – either on paper or mentally, and then talk into a recorder to address each point. Do this in an environment where you feel comfortable. A private room in your home is fine – or you might do this on a long drive if you don't have to think much about where you are going, such as a freeway. Just talk into a mike and record your thoughts. Later, select, organize, and edit this material.

- **<u>Using Automatic Writing</u>**. Automatic writing is like talking to yourself, except you write as the thoughts come to you. Give yourself a topic from your book outline to start with, and start reflecting and writing whatever comes to you. Then go through the usual select, organize, and edit process.

But don't, as one of my clients did, think of the words you have written from automatic writing as channeled for a special purpose or God-given, so you believe you can't change or rewrite anything. My client's instructions to me were to edit but not change any words, because that might change the meaning. So except for some minimal changes for typos and adding some headers and transitions to break-up the text, I left everything in her exact words. She didn't even want me to add some additional lines to summarize her text or to provide an introduction to what she was writing in order to cue an editor or agent into what the book was about. Rather she wanted readers to discover that for themselves. Unfortunately, the result of her determination to keep everything as it was supposedly "given" to her was an unpublishable book.

- **<u>Just Write It!</u>** You might also organize your material into an introduction and chapters, and start writing. This method works best if you have already done other book writing and are good at organizing information in your mind, so you can write in an organized way.

You can use any combination of these methods, though it is better to use a particular method for an individual chapter, so everything you want to organize for that chapter is there in one place, rather than having to integrate and weave together information from different sources.

I typically use the "Just Write It!" method, since I have written many books before and am able to organize an outline in my mind mentally. I can also write fairly tightly to begin with, so I have to do minimal editing. But if you are new to doing books, I would suggest using one of the other methods or working with a professional ghostwriter or co-writer, who knows how to shape your material from your notes, workshops, seminars, interviews, or self-talk notes.

Publishing And Distributing Your E-Book

While one format for publishing an e-book is a PDF, there are a growing number of electronic formats, such as Kindle. All you need is a Word document to start with and then the software for that platform will convert your document into the format needed for that platform.

In fact, there are now e-book publishers, such as SmashWords (www. smashwords.com) who will take your Word document and convert it into numerous electronic formats, though you may have to simplify the Word formatting, such as by normalizing the text, getting rid of extra spacing, and converting any large headlines to no longer than a 14 point standard font like Times Roman or Courier. Currently, once it's properly formatted, SmashWords will take your Word document and convert it into 9 platforms at no charge to you. You set the price you want, and they will pay you 85% of what they collect.

For this type of publishing, publishers recommend that you keep the price low – under $10, and preferably around $3 to $5. The reason for this is there is customer resistance to paying more than $10 for an e-book. But even with the lower price, you will probably end up making more because of the increased volume, rather than selling at a higher price. The high prices for some e-books is only possible for certain types of books with specialized information, as previously noted, such as the book on how to make money on the internet or how to save an amazing amount of money on your mortgage. For most books, set a low price as an incentive to buy.

Generally, if you do put your book out as an e-book, you still have to do extensive promotion to get it noticed and entice people to buy. There are at least 200,000 e-books published each year, in addition to about 200,000 bound books. So you have to do something to stand out, using the various PR techniques described in this book, from doing social media marketing and traditional PR to putting on workshops and seminars.

Finding A Mainstream Publisher

Once you have built up enough credibility and sales with your e-books or print-on-demand books, you have a more powerful platform for finding to a mainstream publishing company to take over your book so you get even wider distribution. You will also be more likely to get a larger advance when a mainstream publisher expresses interest, since you now have a proven product, because you have already shown there is a market for your book. So instead of getting a more common $5-15,000 advance for a nonfiction book or first novel, you may get a bigger deal, say $50,000 to $100,000 – sometimes even more.

CHAPTER 11:
CREATING A PACKAGE
OF MATERIALS

Besides your e-book, you can create additional materials that help to build your credibility and authority. Plus you can gain more income by selling them and/or use them as part of your promotion. These extra materials can include audiobooks, videos, workbooks, and other materials sold separately or packaged together.

USING AUDIOBOOKS AND VIDEOS

Since some people like to get their information through an audiobook, especially if they like to listen while they drive, you can turn your written book into an audio book. Or you might start with an audio book and turn that into a written book.

One way to turn an e-book into an audio book is to read it aloud or use an actor who does voice-over work. Or tape a workshop, teleseminar, or webinar, and do a light edit, such as by adding an introduction and close for each session.

You can also use this content to create a video. While you might start by reading it aloud, add interesting visual images to keep the viewer involved.

These could include animated illustrations, a collage of still photos, or actors acting out some scenes from the book.

Another approach is to set up video cameras at a workshop or seminar and videotape that; then have it edited to create a professional looking product, with titles, music, and other elements that make a high quality video.

CREATING A COMBINATION PACKAGE

Increasingly, people are creating combo packages they can both sell and use to promote what they are doing.

Such combo packages include print-on-demand or regular books, workbooks, videos, audios, sample products, advertising materials like postcards, and other materials.

When you package these materials, use a logo, unifying slogan, or title to create a brand image and name for your company. By sharing a similar look and logo, that helps to identify you.

A prime example of this includes Donald Trump, who at one time was just another real estate promoter. But now he has the Trump logo on a TV show *The Apprentice,* university, multilevel health foods company, on books, on tapes, on workshop materials, and more.

CHAPTER 12:
NETWORKING EVENTS

Another way to promote your product or service is through networking events. Despite all the attention to social media and having virtual presence, nothing beats actually meeting people personally.

CREATING YOUR OWN NETWORKING EVENTS

Creating your own networking events is a way to create even more of a presence than just going to events. It will also add to your expertise and credibility. There are now some easy ways to build interest through using the social media, like LinkedIn and FaceBook, and through online networking groups like MeetUp.

Some Examples of Successful Events

For example, one man who has put on networking events in L.A., Chicago, Phoenix, and other cities, created a lot of contacts through LinkedIn. So before he even came to L.A. where he launched his first events, he already had over 500 contacts. Then, he invited these contacts to networking events at hotels and clubs in these cities. These events started off with 20-30 attendees paying $10 in advance and $15 at the door. Then, as he continued to have these events each month, the number of attendees gradually grew to 30-40 people per events.

Similarly, when I first came to L.A. to get into the film industry, I knew almost no one. But I started some potluck parties at the pool on the roof of my apartment building and announced these events as the assistant organizer of a Hollywood Industry Meetup group. The first event had about 35 people, and as I joined and took over other Meetup groups, I announced these events on them. Eventually, I had about 100-150 people coming to these events each month. In turn, these events provided a great forum for announcing various projects I was involved in and finding clients for some of my services.

Organizing Your Own Social Event

Putting on such social events adds that all-important personal touch. So besides whatever you do online through the social media, you might set up some house parties or sales parties where you invite people to network with each other. Plan on about two hours for these events. Have a sign-up table where you collect business cards, names, and e-mails. Spend a little time about half-way through the event giving a brief introduction to your product or service. And if you have others help you or have contributions from sponsors at these events, give them an opportunity to briefly introduce themselves and their companies, too. You might even have some tables for sponsors where they can provide information to attendees.

Setting Up a Promotional Workshop or Seminar

Another good way to introduce yourself and any books, products or services you offer is to organize a workshop or seminar on this topic. A common approach is to put on an introductory meeting that's free or at most $5 to $10 to get the word out about you and what you do. Pick a topic that will appeal to your likely customer by offering to help them in some way.

Then, when people attend, you can talk a little about your books, products, or services, even offer some for sale – ideally at a discount to encourage purchases now, and offer more in-depth workshops or seminars for which you can charge more.

For instance, one man doing workshops on the social media promoted these events through LinkedIn social networking events he advertised and gave a brief presentation about his workshops. He also attended events others organized and gave 15-20 minute talks on how to best use the social media for promotional purposes and then offered a workshop for people who wanted to do more. Typically, his LinkedIn events in the L.A. area attracted 30 to 40 attendees, and then his workshops on using LinkedIn were attended by 15-20 people for $50 to $75 each. Another man offered free programs with tips on using the Internet to increase one's business and invited people to an advanced workshop on successful Internet strategies for $250-500, which attracted about a dozen attendees.

So think about how you might organize your own program related to the book, product, or service for which you are seeking customers or clients. People are more likely to come if this first meeting is free. Then, you can use this meeting as a forum to invite people to attend your workshop or seminar or sell your products or services. You can increase the number of people who sign up or buy if you offer a special price for those signing up or buying at this meeting – such as 20-50% off your usual price.

Attending Networking Events

When you go to networking events have a short introductory greeting prepared. This greeting is what's commonly called an "elevator pitch," because that's how long you might spend talking to somebody in an elevator -- about 10-30 seconds for your initial meeting. Then, if the person you talk to seems interested, you can say a little more, as well as ask the person about his product or service.

It's helpful to practice your elevator speech of various lengths – 10, 15, and 30 seconds, so when you meet somebody you can quickly get to the point and get your message across.

In some cases, you might be able to make a small presentation to the whole group at these networking events, and commonly you will have 30 seconds or at most a minute. To make the best presentation, work up a short introduction you might give to the whole group, which should be a little more formal than the brief spur-of-the moment conversational exchange you might have. By planning and practicing in advance, you'll know exactly what to say.

Being Prepared Anytime

Besides going to organized networking events, look for opportunities to present a brief introduction to your product or service anytime. For example, if you talk to someone while you are shopping or sit next to a receptive seatmate in the airport, on a bus, or on a train, you might be able to do a short pitch after a brief exchange of pleasantries.

So always be ready to say something. If you have some small samples you can carry with you, take them along; I know people in a number of companies who bring out their samples when appropriate. The way to do this is to look for an opportunity during a conversation to steer it around to a related topic; then you mention how your product or service has helped others or might help the person you are talking to. And then if the person seems interested, you bring out your sample product, some information about it, or you invite the person to go to an opportunity or sales meeting to learn more.

But a caution. If people seem to be tuning out on your presentation, don't keep going. Some salespeople do, and it is very off-putting.

A Caution on Promoting MLM Products and Services

I have found this over-promotion or inappropriate promotion most apt to be a problem with multi-level salespeople. Sometimes they are so into their product that they think everybody they talk to will want to jump on board to not only get the product but to get an early start in the MLM pyramid structure to increase their chances of making a lot of money marketing the product. So these salespeople overdo it by aggressively pushing on and on in promoting their product. But this approach is not only likely to push a not-interested consumer even further away, but it can wear out a friendship.

Thus, don't overenthusiastically pitch people on buying a product or getting into the marketing program. Generally, it's better to approach building a sales team more slowly. This way, you see people as potential customers first. Then if people like the product AND want to consider marketing it, tell them about the marketing plan and income potential. Commonly, if you are promoting a really good product, you will find that only about 5-10% of customers want to also market the product or service. So focus your attention on helping those people who really do want to participate in the business, rather than trying to recruit everyone into becoming a marketer and promoter, too.

Otherwise, you'll waste a lot of time signing up and trying to work with people who don't have the energy, time, or commitment to market the product. And if most of the people you recruit are getting in because they want to market the product or service and have little or no interest in using the product or service, the program will to turn into a pyramid scheme. In this case, there is relatively little interest in buying or using the product; the main interest is on marketing it. If so, you will eventually run out of prospective recruits, because a growing number of people you contact are already in the program. And no one will make much money, because relatively few people are actually buying the products, which is the source of the commissions, because in any legitimate MLM program, you can't make money from the marketing materials or fees paid by people to market the program.

In short, choose to only represent and promote products and services which you truly feel are valuable whether or not there is a marketing opportunity. And figure that only 5-10 percent of any customers will be interested in marketing and promoting the product. Instead, most people will be customers for a highly credible product or service, and they will want to buy even if it is sold through regular retail channels, rather than via MLM.

Participating in Referral Clubs

Another great marketing and promotional tool is referral clubs, such as BNI, which stands for Business Network International, or LeTip. These two groups are among the largest of such organizations, which chapters all over the U.S. and internationally. Also, you'll find a number of locally based referral groups or smaller national groups. I've been a member of BNI, which has about 3800 chapters worldwide, for about five years.

In these referral or leads groups, the usual policy is to have members from different fields, who attend weekly meetings, usually for an early breakfast. Each member does a short pitch of about 30 seconds in which they introduce themselves and their companies and state what kind of referral they are most interested in getting. Then, people give each other referrals and share about the business they have gotten as a result of a referral. Typically, these groups have 20 to 40 members, each with a different types of business.

Come prepared to exchange business cards, and bring along any flyers or brochures to display or hand out.

<u>Participating in Entrepreneurial Organizations, Conferences, and Meetings</u>

You can also do networking, marketing, and promotion through organizations of entrepreneurs and at the conferences, workshops, and seminars put on by these groups.

One such group is CEOSpace, which has a lot of networking events to sign up people for their quarterly training programs which feature dozens of speakers talking about strategies for success. The event is fairly pricey -- $7500 for the conference and a lifetime membership in the organization, with a discount for additional people from your organization. Other groups similarly have these networking events for assorted workshops and seminars.

Even if you aren't interested in signing up for these more expensive programs, you may find the networking very valuable. But if networking is your primarily intent, carefully consider or tune out their sales pitch. These expensive conferences, seminars, and workshops do well for some people. But they aren't for everyone, especially if you are seeking more clients, rather than learning how to build and promote your business from the speakers. That's because the people you will meet at these expensive programs are the same kind of people attending these networking events, and they are primarily seeking funding and clients for their own programs.

Certainly, if you have discretionary income of your own to spend, it's worth taking the chance that you will find the clients or funds if you go. But if you have to borrow or beg funds from others to attend, which one local group organizer kept urging me to do so I could attend their $7500 conference, claiming I would see all the people I needed at the event to quickly get back the money I needed to pay back any loans, this can be a big risk. While some people may make enough money by attending to compensate for their investment, not everyone does. It's like investing in high risk but lucrative stocks. You could make a lot, but there are no guarantees and you could lose a lot, too. So you have to carefully weigh the costs and assess whether it is worth it to take the risk that the program will be very worthwhile for you, because the group members sometimes oversell the value of these programs, as many attendees have discovered.

Getting Tables at Networking Events and Conferences

At some networking events and conferences, you may have an opportunity to showcase your product or service at a table as an exhibitor or sponsor, and this can be a way to stand out and get more clients and business. Typically, tables are 6 feet long and about $50-150 at many local events; about $500-1500 at regional and national events. And sometimes you can share a table with somebody else to cut down on your costs. This can work especially well if you can share with someone in a complimentary field, such as when someone in real estate teams up with a mortgage broker.

Depending on your product or service, it may be worth it to have your own table or share one. Figure out what you are likely to make at the event and through future sales to decide if being an exhibitor or sponsor is worth it for you.

While you might have some sales at these events, especially if you selling an impulse product, such as jewelry, generally regard having a table as a place to make contacts and collect business cards, so you can follow up afterwards. A good way to collect these cards is to have a prize drawing from the business cards you collect to inspire people to stop by your booth and give you their cards. When you do this, it's good to give out a prize that would appeal to someone interested in your type of business. That'll help to screen out people who might give you their card just because of the possibility of winning a prize, though they are not a good prospect for your business.

The main types of businesses making sales at these events are those with impulse items that are not generally available elsewhere, such as jewelry. Or you may be able to spark sales with a special promotion, such as offering half off for a new digital camera or giving away a free one or two months' subscription for those who subscribe for a year and sign up now.

However you collect any business cards, follow-up within a few days to two weeks after the event, so it is fresh in people's minds.

CHAPTER 13:
USING THE SOCIAL
MEDIA

The social media has become another powerful way to get out your message. In fact it is so important, that it deserves its own book, and I will be writing a book on using this for PR.

The Major Social Media Sites

Today, the most popular sites are LinkedIn, Facebook, and Twitter, though a number of new sites are growing in popularity such as Twitter. Also, there are some specialized social media sites devoted to a particular profession, such as RedRoom for authors.

Of all the social media sites, LinkedIn has become the most popular for making business connections. Facebook is most noted for making personal connections, and Twitter has become something of a quick instant message service.

The Importance of Building a Relationship

While some marketers start off by immediately promoting some new product or service, this can be a quick way for people to think you are spamming them. Instead, social media experts recommend that you start a conversation to build relationships by showing interest in what others are doing and posting helpful information that would appeal to those who are linked to or following you. For instance, you might post comments about interesting new books and videos or helpful articles. This way you engage in an ongoing dialogue with others in the group that helps to build trust.

Then, after building the relationship and developing some trust, you will be better able to get positive interest when you post information about your book, product, service, or events you are involved in. Or even better, a question may come up about using a product or service that you offer, and you can naturally answer by describing your product or service and how it can help. In turn, people will be more receptive to this information from you, because you have taken the time to build up a relationship. You haven't just come into the group with a product or service to promote right away, which could be off-putting.

Posting Your Information on Multiple Sites

Besides posting information about what you are doing on individual sites from time to time, you can use ping.fm to simultaneously post this information on several social media sites. You have to first belong to these sites and set up a profile on each one. But once you do, you can then send out – or ping -- your information at the same time to each site. You just note which sites to include at ping.fm.

Joining Groups in Your Field

Another way to leverage the number of people you contact when you post information is to join the relevant interest groups on each of these sites. For instance, if you are a writer, you will find various publishing, writing, and book groups you can join on LinkedIn or Facebook. If you are in the film, entertainment, or music industries, you will find dozens of groups in those fields. Just put in the categories you find of interest in the search box for that social media sites and ask to join any of those groups. Generally, you will be enrolled as a matter of course.

You can also start your own group on these sites. Then, invite others already in your social network on these sites to join. You can also invite other people you meet to join, as well as to link to you individually.

<u>Combining the Social Media with Other Networking</u>

Besides joining or starting your own social media groups, you can join or start your own group on social networking sites like Meetup. While these sites are designed for personal networking, there's a good synergy with the social media sites, because you can use the social media to indicate the networking events you are going to or the meetings you are organizing yourself. And if you are organizing workshops and seminars to promote what you are doing, you can use the social media to invite people to these events.

You might also combine using social media and networking sites with personal networking. For instance, you might go to some of the networking events that are promoted through LinkedIn, Facebook, or Meetup, just as you might go to a regular networking event such as put on by your local Chamber of Commerce or to a trade show. Then, when you got to these events, you can network with both the people in the booths and the attendees. Bring along your flyers to hand uts and your business cards. Then, as you go around the event, if anybody has a need for what you're doing, hand them a flyer and/or business card, get a card from them, and follow up after that. Besides phoning or sending e-mails, you can invite them to join you on the most popular social media sites liked LinkedIn, Facebook, or Twitter, too.

CHAPTER 14: WORKING WITH OTHERS IN YOUR PR CAMPAIGN

DOING JOINT PR WITH OTHERS

Another approach to PR is doing joint promotions with other people. This joint PR approach can work well if you have complimentary products or services and want to contact the same target market. You might think of yourself as "Power Partners".

For example, you might send out releases for guest appearances and interviews that include information about both of you. Or you might plan a jointly produced event or special, which you promote together, such as when MacDonald's promotes having a "Happy Meal" and getting a special toy from a partner company, such as Hasbro, as a prize.

If you are both doing speaking, workshops, or promoting books, you can set up an event where you both are presenters and share the costs of publicizing the event.

Another good way to do joint PR is to share the costs of some promotional event or activity. For instance, you might share a trade show together, so instead of you each paying for a full booth, you pay half and your partner pays the other half. A further perk is that you have someone's who's in the booth to meet potential clients or customers while you go around the show; then you can take your turn in the booth, whle the other person goes around the show.

Then, too, you might share PR services or database access as partners, so you split the costs. Commonly, in this case, you will both share a single password, so you have to work out times when you can each access the service, much like a company may arrange for several different staffers to use the account at different times.

USING AND CHOOSING A PR PROFESSIONAL

If you are going to hire a PR professional, assess what they have done in the past, what they will do for you, and what the cost will be.

Making Your Decision

To decide who to hire, consider what each PR person proposes as their approach to your PR campaign. Consider if their vision appeals to you, or if not, see how flexible are they to making changes to implement your vision. Or consider if perhaps their vision might be even better than your original idea; if so, that's a very valuable contribution to improving your campaign.

In particular ask the following:

- What is their track record? What clients have they worked with and with what success? Generally, PR people will want to list their successful clients and campaigns in their literature or on their Websites.

- What have they done for their past clients? Brochures? Press releases? Websites? Personal calls to the media? Trade shows? Special events? Etc. Typically, PR people will have is a portfolio of examples of work for previous clients and a description of their successful results

- What are they proposing to do for you?

- What are the costs for the whole package and for different parts of it?

Besides asking such questions, tell the PR person what your budget is. This way, they can quickly tell you if they can work with your budget or if they can't. Or possibly they might be able to reduce the scope of their program to conform to your budget, or they may show you why you will benefit from increasing your budget, and you may be able to do so.

Cutting Down Your PR Costs in Working with a Pro

A good way to cut down costs, if necessary, in working with a PR person, is to do some of the more routine PR activities to cut down your costs. If the PR person is agreeable, you might do these more routine tasks under the guidance of the PR pro, possibly with the help of an assistant or unpaid intern. Then, the PR person will do the key personal contact and follow-up work.

For instance, I work with a PR pro in LA who works in a small agency and has been successful with numerous clients. We have an agreement where I can occasionally use her database to find contacts in selected categories for an e-mail query. Then, after I do a blast of a PR release to the media, she will do follow-up with anyone who is interested in learning more.

Getting Quotes and Weighing Alternatives

Ideally, get quotes from two or three PR pros and weigh the alternatives. Take into consideration that people with more experience, and therefore more established relationships with contacts in the media, will charge more. Some can be really expensive, charging $3000-5000 a month retainer, sometimes more.

But if you don't have a budget for the more established, expensive pro, it may be worth it to choose someone with less experience who is very eager and will put in the committed personal time to your project. Often the more expensive PR people have a team of people, so they don't do much of the hands-on work -- the members of their staff do. Instead, they spend much of their time supervising the lower level employees or looking for new clients. So you might get even better results while spending less with one of the newer, less experienced and expensive PR pros.

Working with PR People Locally or at a Distance

One consideration that sometimes comes up is whether to work with a PR person you have personally met or select someone you have met on the Internet or spoken to through a referral on the phone.

I personally prefer to actually meet with the person, but a long distance relationship can work quite well. And this may be the only way to find a good PR person, when you are out of town and want to hire a PR person who is more centrally located to the media, which is primarily in New York, LA, and a few other major cities. So having a PR person who is better situated near the media may be a more important consideration than having PR person near you, since you want someone who has easy access to the media and has the advantage of making personal contacts with the media people.

There are some people who use outsourcing to hire people to do their PR, since they can hire people for much less to contact the media over the Internet, such as by sending out multiple letters for you by e-mail. These costs are much reduced, since you can find people in India, Pakistan, and other countries such as in Eastern Europe and Asia who will charge much less. They may even charge as little as $3 to $5 an hour at the low end to $10-20 an hour at the high end.

But when you outsource work, you have to be very specific on what you want these distant employees to do and limit them to doing routine work, such as posting your copy or links on LinkedIn or Facebook.

You can even hire employees or interns to act like you in posting promotional information, which I have done, using a couple of students and interns. But you have to carefully direct them and check what they are doing, so they don't express something in a different way than you would or do things you don't want them to do. You also have to check to make sure they don't do something that is ineffective, such as engaging in an e-mail exchange with someone who may be responsive but is not really going to be a client or customer for your services or products. Such ongoing contact with such non-prospects online can turn into a real time-waster, unless you are careful and direct your employees to do what's most effective.

Thus, while it's fine to hire people at a low cost with little or no experience for doing the routine work, for the personal PR, you want somebody who has a track record and knows what he or she is doing. And ideally you can meet with any prospective PR person, so you have a personal connection and feel comfortable that whoever you are hiring can do a good job.

CHAPTER 15:
ASSESSING YOUR PR
CAMPAIGN

The Importance Of Timing

Timing your PR is especially critical. Even if you appear on Oprah, which does wonders for book authors, it's not a magic bullet if your book isn't widely available when the show airs. People will go on to the next thing if your book isn't immediately available in the bookstores or through Amazon.

That's what I discovered when I was an expert guest on Oprah, Montel Williams, and several other shows, because of my book called THE TRUTH ABOUT LYING. The book had come out about two years before, and at the time my publicist sent a release to Oprah's producer and to many other shows. But the information just sat in the files for two years until the Jim Carrey film *Liar, Liar* came out, resulting in a sudden upsurge of interest in the subject.

On Oprah, five people were selected to represent the different types of liars described in the book, and I was suppose to comment on these different liars and their stories. And on the other shows I commented on the results of lie detector tests and on assessing the truth of conflict tales by different guests. So these shows would have been a great promotional opportunity. But the book was no longer in the vast majority of book stores. Thus, while a few people were able to track down a few copies still in stores or call me to get a copy, the PR splash was essentially wasted. That's because unless a book or other product is in the stores, all that publicity doesn't matter much. I did use my appearances to put together a short video with clips from the shows that helped me in the future. But for selling books, the timing was off, since the book was no longer in general circulation.

BEING READY TO RESPOND AND MAKE NEEDED CHANGES

Thus, if you are going to be doing promotion, be sure you have the logistics of distribution worked out so you have your book or product readily available, whether in retail stores or online, so people can easily go into stores to pick it up or order online. Or if you plan to have automated sales with e-mail responses or website auto-responders, make sure that's all in place. In short, when you kick off your PR campaign, you have to be ready to respond.

KEEPING TRACK OF YOUR PR RESULTS

You also want to be ready to track your results to make sure people are responding to your PR campaign. This way you can quickly make necessary changes, if you find a particular campaign is not working.

Deciding If Your Campaign Is Working or Not

I assessed such campaign responses when I was selling my business. Before I made the decision to sell, I hired a publicist to promote the company, which was called "Making Connections," since it was designed to connect individuals to book publishers and agents, the film industry, the media, and the music, game, and other industries.

She started doing PR to the major local media, with a goal of getting a feature in the Los Angeles Times or either of the Santa Monica papers, where I was then living. But she had a number of restrictions since she was doing hands-on local PR, rather than sending out an e-mail blast, as I did through the News Media Connection. For instance, she didn't want to pitch two people simultaneously who edited the Santa Monica papers, since an article could only be published in one paper, and she didn't want to anger one editors by saying the other editor had already picked up the story. Also, she wanted to wait to contact them, so she could see if she could get an article in the *LA*

Times first, because if a local paper published the story first, the *LA Times* wouldn't pick it up; though the local papers might be interested in a follow-up article with a local angle after the story ran in the *LA Times*.

However, after she started promoted the service, she discovered that the editors at all the papers found the story too commercial to pick up. They felt it was appropriate for advertising, but not for a story. As a result, she didn't get any press coverage, despite her hard work in repeatedly calling the media to follow-up.

Thus, after a few weeks, I realized that this was not an effective PR campaign, although I had gotten articles in the *Wall Street Journal* and *Contra Costa Times* about my business several years earlier that led to several dozen new customers after each article. That's what made me think I only needed another article to make the company take off again. But this didn't happen, because, as I now realized, when these earlier articles appeared this was a new type of business, using e-mail queries to pitch books and other projects for clients. But now this idea was no longer really new, plus I was in LA which is a much harder market in which to get noticed than when I was based in Oakland.

But once I realized from my publicist's reports that this campaign wasn't working well, I was able to quickly drop the campaign and cut my losses, rather than trying to pitch the same business with a different angle. Also, instead of trying to get more customers, I decided to sell the business instead. So my strategy shifted to finding a business broker and helping that broker promote the sale of the business – and after three months, I was able to sell the business.

Thus, consider the initial weeks of the campaign like a test launch, where you see if it works. If not, you have to be ready to end a campaign and cut your losses when you can.

Ways to Track Your Results

To track the results of your campaign, keep a list of your any press coverage if you get featured on TV and radio, or in newspapers, magazines, or the online media. Some things to keep track of include the following. Get as much information as you can.

- What stations or shows you were on, the name of the host and/or producer, contact information, and the size of the audience for that station or show;

- What publications included articles about you and the circulation of that publication.

Then, besides using this to see how well your campaign is going, you can include this information in your kit on a page or two which features the press you got. Use a header such as "Featured on..." and then list the coverage you got. Organize it by category (ie: newspapers, magazines, TV) if you have more than seven or eight items or several items in each category. Otherwise, combine the different categories together. In either case, highlight the most important news media first and try to keep your list to one page or back-to-back page.

CHECKING THE TRAFFIC TO YOUR WEBSITE

If you have included a link to your Website in your press materials, this is another way to check the effectiveness of your campaign. You should see an increase in your Website traffic.

You can find out information on your traffic from month to month from your Website hosting company or by putting your Website name in a service that does a Website traffic analysis, such as Google Analytics.

For example, the Hostcentric Website server, which I use for a dozen sites, has a "Check Traffic" link from the control panel. After I follow that link, I can click on the "Visitor's Statistics" link and update that and then get a report with the latest data. This traffic report provides a summary of month by month traffic, along with the daily average of people who come to the website and the numbers of visits. You can also get special programs that give you a more detailed report, such as where the visitors come from as referrals from other sites, like Google or Yahoo, or the countries where they are from. You can also see in graphic form how the number of unique visitors and visits changes from day to day, week to week, month to month, or years to year.

THE COSTS OF A PR CAMPAIGN

The advantage of doing your own PR is it is much less expensive than working with a PR person. There are no guarantees either way, but you will spend less.

Different Types of Arrangements

When you do your own PR, figure on spending about $400-700 to get access to a current database of media contacts, such as through CornerBar PR. Then you can send out press releases or call the contacts you select.

If you are going to do mass mailings to the different media – say 100 or more in a media category – you can get customer management or bulk mail software like Group Mail for about $400. Then, you export the information from the database in a .csv or Excel format and import it into the software program to mail it out. For quantity mailings, you will also need access to a dedicated mail server, such as through Peer 1 for about $400-500 a month. If you are going to do a continuing media campaign for over three or four months, it may be worth it to make an investment of about $2000, which averages out to about $500 a month, less than the cost of the average retainer for a PR person – about $1500-3000 a month, sometimes more.

Should you use a service like News Media Connection or the PR and Networking Connection to send out your release, you don't need to invest in any special software yourself. Instead, the cost is determined by the number of media categories contacted, ranging from about $250 for one category with several hundred to several thousand contacts to $1000 for a complete media blast to 15,000-20,000 contacts. The costs of using a service like PR Web, PRNewswire, or BusinessWire might be about the same or more, depending on who you want to contact.

If you hire a PR person, you will typically pay a retainer of about $1000-3000 a month, though some top PR people charge $4000-5000. When I did PR for my business for two months, I found someone who was fairly new and she gave me an introductory price of $1,000, though most PR people would charge $3,000 to 5,000 for a retainer for what she did.

There are also some PR people who work on a placement fee instead of an hourly rate, so they get about $100 per interview arranged. The downside here, though, is that you might end up paying for interviews on small radio stations or for articles in local and regional papers and magazines. So your costs may run up, though you get little economic return for the placements.

The Duration and Costs of a PR Campaign

Generally, most PR campaigns have a window of 3 to 4 months. This allows about a month to set up the theme and message of your campaign, write a press release, and prepare any supplementary materials, such as "Questions for Interviews" and a personal or company bio.

The release and initial phone contact is typically timed to occur about 6 weeks to 2 months before the product comes out on the market – with a longer lead time of about 2-3 months for magazines and about 1-2 weeks for newspapers, radio, and the Internet. Then the campaign usually continues for about 6 weeks to 2 months after the initial release.

Thus, when you hire a publicist on a retainer, figure on about 4-5 months, unless you decide to cancel the campaign early as I did.

Depending on the size of the retainer and length of the campaign, figure on about $4000-$25,000 for a campaign using a professional, though there are no guarantees the PR campaign will work. Obviously, doing your own PR will be much less than that.

DOING A COST BENEFIT ANALYIS

After you launch your PR campaign, do this cost benefit analysis to see how well things are working and if you are getting PR results that are worth the investment.

Factors to Consider

Look at how much you are spending for your PR vs. what this campaign is producing. Don't only look at the number of articles or interviews you get with the media. Also, notice if these publications or appearances are turning into getting new clients or sales.

Say you are spending $1,000 a month for a PR person or your own mailings to the media, are you getting more than $1,000 in results?

Take into consideration all of your expenses for whatever PR you're doing. For instance, if you have to fly somewhere to do a TV show, take the total cost into consideration. Commonly, the media will pay for your cost of the flight and your additional travel expenses, such as for tolls and parking. They may even pay for your hotel and meals. But sometimes they don't because of cut backs, so they may only want people in their area, unless your pay for your own travel expenses. But even if the media pays for your out-of-pocket expenses, consider your other costs, such as the number of hours you are spending traveling to and doing the interview and what you would otherwise get paid for that time if you had work. If you can arrange for phone or local on-camera interviews that's great, but otherwise, figure you may have to spend a day or two in travel-time for a few minutes on air.

When I was on Oprah, for instance, they flew me in on one day, I stayed overnight in a hotel, and I was on air for about 15 minutes on two segments. Then, I spent the next day flying home. So you have to ask yourself: even if the program is paying for all of your costs and you feel like a celebrity for that half hour or so, what is the cost of taking that time to be on that show? Is that worth it?

The Length of Time for the Assessment

How long to decide if the campaign is working? Generally, figure on about 2 to 4 months, but be realistic in giving the campaign enough time to work. Usually, that means monitoring what you are doing and your expectations to see if your media pitches are on track. Then, once they go out and you or your PR person makes contact my mail or phone, start assessing the results in the third month, since typically you want to plan a 2-3 months campaign. The first month is generally devoted to getting your materials together, including setting the campaign theme and preparing your press materials, Websites, flyers, brochures, or other information. The second month begins the process, and by the third month, you should be able to see how things are going and evaluate it.

In making your assessment, take into consideration the different response times for the different media. For example, if you get on a TV show, that will usually translate into immediate responses from prospective clients or sales from customers. People see the book or product you are promoting. Then, they buy it or not. By contrast, radio tends to work best with repetition over several weeks. As people hear your ad repeated, they become more persuaded to respond – and often people need to write down or remember this information, because they are listening while they are doing something else, most notably driving in their car.

As for print, what works best is including a call to action in your promotional or advertising copy. Take into consideration the lead time between your article or interview and the actual appearance of your article or interview. Start the evaluation time-clock after it appears.

If interested, people will commonly respond in a day or two after they read an article about you or your book or product. Though sometimes people may store an article for days, weeks, months, or even a year or two, until they are ready to use your product or service.

For example, when articles appeared about me in the *Wall Street Journal* and the *Contra Costa Times* about a business I then owned that connected writers to publishers and agents, within a day or two, I had about 30 responses for each article, and over the next few months, I had another 10-20 prospective clients contact me. In a few instances, a person who saved the article called over a year later, since he or she had now written the book and was finally ready to look for a publisher and agent.

Making Your Decision

After you make your assessment, you can decide what ads or PR strategies to continue and what to drop. Or perhaps you might vary the content or hook of an ad or PR release.

As you assess what has worked and what hasn't, you can build on your successes to determine the next phase of your campaign and cut your losses in stopping what isn't working.

CHAPTER 16:
EXPANDING YOUR PR CAMPAIGN

USING THE PR YOU GET TO GAIN ADDITIONAL MEDIA EXPOSURE

Besides doing an assessment of how well your campaign is going, you can use what you have already done to do more in the future in the following ways:

- collect any articles that appear in magazines, newspapers, or online,

- note who has interviewed you for radio and when that interview will be aired,

- download or purchase tapes of your best radio interviews.

- record any TV interviews or use a service to record clips for you; later you can use those clips on a promotional video as well as post them on your Website, subject to the show's guidelines about the use of such clips (or use them until the show objects; you can always take the video clip down when asked – and commonly no one will ask you to do this).

- keep a record of any talks, workshops, seminars or other presentations you have done.

By keeping track of your previous media coverage, you can create a press package that combines your major media articles, interviews, guest appearances, talks, workshops, and seminars. You can also highlight your past coverage in your press releases or query letters, post on your Website, include in a CD or DVD, or link to posts about you on other sites. Also, you can include information about in your blog, in articles you post on ezines or other sites, and in announcements to the social media. Making regular postings are important, because as you add new material, it will get picked up by the search engines, such as Google, Yahoo, and Bing. And it will go out on an RSS feed, allowing those who read the feed to comment.

For example, I have an RSS feed linked to my blog on Word Press, which is linked to my Website. Sometimes I have gotten comments praising the article, although some comments are from people promoting a product or service or sending out nonsense words to test links. But if you moderate the blog, nothing can get printed on your Website unless you approve. So you can easily delete any spam or promotional comments.

CREATING A UNIQUE IDENTITY FOR YOUR COMPANY

In crafting your PR campaign, it's important to create an identity or branding for your company, product, or service, so you stand out. To this end, ask yourself: What do you do that's unique or different? Then, incorporate that into a brief line of text or logo that's memorable.

Sometimes you will also be more likely to get PR if you position yourself as an expert who can answer questions about something in the news, so people will call on you to comment as an authority. Then, when they introduce you, they will normally indicate your company, book, or other special achievement, and you may get to give contact information at the end. Or the station or publication will keep your contact information on file, so they can refer anyone who wants to reach you directly to you.

CHAPTER 17:
WHEN TO CUT BACK
YOUR PR

While getting the most press you can is ideal, sometimes it is not realistic to do a major campaign, because you have more of a niche book, product, or service, or because you have a message, product, or service that is widely available from other sources. Then, it may make more sense to use advertising or target any PR to a more limited market.

PROMOTING THE UNDIFFERENTIATED PRODUCT OR SERVICE

If you have a book, product, or service that's hard to differentiate, it may be best to do a limited, local campaign.

For example, one client at a workshop asked how to promote his all-in-one Internet marketing service. He pointed out that some companies focus on search engine marketing, others on web design, still others in the social media. But his company had experience in all areas, so, as he explained: "We do everything in house as a one stop shop. You don't have to be in five different companies to get everything you want."

But unfortunately, many other companies could make a similar claim. So it would be hard to differentiate such services in doing PR. A similar problem affects authors of self-help books, who claim to have a slightly different slant, but the perception of the media is likely to be that this is just another book with personal improvement tips.

Thus, if you are doing something that many other people are doing, it is difficult to create your own identity and differentiate yourself to make your company stand out. So it probably wouldn't be worth it to put on an extensive PR campaign or hire a publicist, because it would be really expensive and you would be likely to get a limited return.

Instead, it might make more sense to do your own limited PR directed towards a particular audience, such as in your local area, because then you do have an advantage of being close to your potential customers. Besides targeting the media, you might also join and participate in special interest groups, particularly those in your area, such as through LinkedIn or Meetup. Or create an informational blog or post articles on ezines and other Websites, where you provide potential customers with useful information that might encourage them to buy your product, use your service, or get your book.

PROMOTING THE SPECIALIZED PRODUCT OR SERVICE

If you have a specialized book, product, or service, this is not the kind of thing that is likely to be picked up by the mass media, though you might do well targeting people who write about that niche market.

For instance, in the case of the company offering a number of Internet and Website services, the company might target people who are doing Internet columns, magazines, blogs, or radio shows on Internet topics. And since a number of people offer such services, the company might offer an informational piece about the growing number of people who provide a similar service, and include bio and contact information as part of this piece.

OTHER BOOKS
BY THE AUTHOR

Here are other books on achieving success or improving work relationships by the author:

- *WANT IT, SEE IT, GET IT! VISUALIZE YOUR WAY TO SUCCESS*
- *ENJOY: 101 LITTLE THINGS TO ADD FUN TO YOUR WORK EVERYDAY*
- *LET'S HAVE A SALES PARTY*
- *SUCCESS IN MLM, NETWORK MARKETING, AND PERSONAL SELLING*
- *17 TOP SECRETS FOR HOW TO KEEP YOUR JOB OR FIND NEW WORK TODAY*
- *30 DAYS TO A MORE POWERFUL MEMORY*
- *DISAGREEMENTS, DISPUTES, AND ALL-OUT WAR*
- *A SURVIVAL GUIDE FOR WORKING WITH HUMANS*
- *A SURVIVAL GUIDE FOR WORKING WITH BAD BOSSES*
- *A SURVIVAL GUIDE TO MANAGING EMPLOYEES FROM HELL*
- *HOW TO COLLECT THE MONEY PEOPLE OWE YOU*

AUTHOR CONTACT INFORMATION

Here's how to contact the author for information about other books and about speaking for your organization or putting on workshops and seminars for your organization:

Gini Graham Scott, Ph.D.
Director
Changemakers
6114 La Salle, #358
Oakland, CA 94611
(510) 339-1625 ; Fax : (510) 339-1626
changemakers@pacbell.net
www.ginigrahamscott.com

Or visit Gini Graham Scott's Websites for her books:

www.findworkwithgini.com (featuring *17 Top Secrets for How to Keep Your Job or Find New Work Today*
www.letshaveasalesparty.com (featuring books on party plan selling)
www.workwithgini.com (books on improving work relationships)
www.wantitseeitgetit.com (featuring *Want It, See It, Get It!*)
www.enjoythebook.com (featuring *Enjoy! 101 Little Ways to Add Fun to Your Work Everyday*
www.badbosses.net (featuring *A Survival Guide for Working with Bad Bosses)*
www.workingwithhumans.com (featuring *A Survival Guide for Working with Humans, A Survival Guide to Managing Employees from Hell,* and *Disagreements, Disputes, and All Out War)*

www.ingramcontent.com/pod-product-compliance
Lightning Source LLC
Chambersburg PA
CBHW071231170526
45165CB00003B/1064

* 9 781450 204606 *